The Women of England: Their Social Duties and Domestic Habits

Mrs. Ellis

THE WOMEN OF ENGLAND, THEIR SOCIAL DUTIES, AND
DOMESTIC HABITS.

BY

MRS. ELLIS,

AUTHOR OF "THE POETRY OF LIFE, " "PICTURES OF PRIVATE
LIFE, " ETC.

1839

PREFACE.

AT a time when the pressure of stirring events, and the urgency of public and private interests, render it increasingly desirable that every variety of labour should be attended with an immediate and adequate return; I feel that some apology is necessary for the presumption of inviting the attention of the public to a work, in which I have been compelled to enter into the apparently insignificant detail of familiar and ordinary life.

The often-repeated truth—that "trifles make the sum of human things, " must plead my excuse; as well as the fact, that while our libraries are stored with books of excellent advice on general conduct, we have no single work containing the particular minutiæ of practical duty, to which I have felt myself called upon to invite the consideration of the young women of the present day. We have many valuable dissertations upon female character, as exhibited on the broad scale of virtue; but no direct definition of those minor parts of domestic and social intercourse, which strengthen into habit, and consequently form the basis of moral character.

It is worthy of remark also, that these writers have addressed their observations almost exclusively to ladies, or occasionally to those who hold a subordinate situation under the influence of ladies; while that estimable class of females who might be more specifically denominated women, and who yet enjoy the privilege of liberal education, with exemption from the pecuniary necessities of labour, are almost wholly overlooked.

It is from a high estimate of the importance of this class in upholding the moral worth of our country, that I have addressed my remarks especially to them; and in order to do so with more effect, I have ventured to penetrate into the familiar scenes of domestic life, and have thus endeavoured to lay bare some of the causes which frequently lie hidden at the root of general conduct.

Had I not known before the commencement of this work, its progress would soon have convinced me, that in order to perform my task with candour and faithfulness, I must renounce all idea of what is called fine writing; because the very nature of the duty I have undertaken, restricts me to the consideration of subjects, too minute in themselves to admit of their being expatiated upon with eloquence by the writer—too familiar to produce upon the reader any startling effect. Had I even felt within myself a capability for treating any subject in this manner, I should have been willing in this instance to resign all opportunity of such display, if, by so doing, I could more clearly point out to my countrywomen, by what means they may best meet that pressing exigency of the times, which so urgently demands a fresh exercise of moral power on their part, to win back to the homes of England, the boasted felicity for which they once were famed.

Anxious as I am to avoid the charge of unnecessary trifling on a subject so serious as the moral worth of the women of England, there is beyond this a consideration of far higher importance, to which I would invite the candid attention of the serious part of the public, while I offer, what appears to me a sufficient apology, for having written a book on the subject of morals, without having made it strictly religious. I should be sorry indeed, if, by so doing, I brought upon myself the suspicion of yielding for one moment to the belief that there is any other sure foundation for good morals, than correct religious principle; but I do believe, that, with the Divine blessing, a foundation may be laid in very early life, before the heart has been illuminated by Divine truth, or has experienced its renovating power, for those domestic habits, and relative duties, which in after life will materially assist the developement of the christian character. And I am the more convinced of this, because we sometimes see, in sincere and devoted Christians, such peculiarities of conduct as materially hinder their usefulness—such early-formed habits, as they themselves would be glad to escape from, but which continue to cling around them in their earthly course, like the clustering of weeds in the traveller's path.

It may perhaps more fully illustrate my view of this important subject, to say that those who would train up young people without the cultivation of moral habits, trusting solely to the future influence of religion upon their hearts, are like mariners, who, while they wait for their bark to be safely guided out to sea, allow their sails to swing idly in the wind, their cordage to become entangled, and the general outfit of their vessel to suffer injury and decay; so that when the pilot comes on board, they lose much of the advantage of his services, and fail to derive the anticipated benefit from his presence.

All that I would venture to recommend with regard to morals, is, that the order and right government of the vessel should, as far as is possible, be maintained, so that when the hope of better and surer guidance is realized, and the heavenly Pilot in his own good time arrives, all things may be ready—nothing out of order, and nothing wanting, for a safe and prosperous voyage.

It is therefore solely to the cultivation of habits that I have confined my attention—to the minor morals of domestic life. And I have done this, because there are so many abler pens than mine employed in teaching and enforcing the essential truths of religion; because there is an evident tendency in society, as it exists in the present day, to overlook these minor points; and because it is impossible for them to be neglected, without serious injury to the Christian character.

SARAH STICKNEY ELLIS.

PENTONVILLE, FEB. 1839.

CONTENTS.

CHAPTER I. CHARACTERISTICS OF THE WOMEN OF ENGLAND.

EVERY country has its peculiar characteristics, not only of climate and scenery, of public institutions, government, and laws; but every country has also its moral characteristics, upon which is founded its true title to a station, either high or low, in the scale of nations.

The national characteristics of England are the perpetual boast of her patriotic sons; and there is one especially, which it behoves all British subjects not only to exult in, but to cherish and maintain. Leaving the justice of her laws, the extent of her commerce, and the amount of her resources, to the orator, the statesman, and the political economist, there yet remains one of the noblest features in her national character, which may not improperly be regarded as within the compass of a woman's understandings and the province of a woman's pen. It is the domestic character of England—the home comforts, and fireside virtues for which she is so justly celebrated. These I hope to be able to speak of without presumption, as intimately associated with, and dependent upon, the moral feelings and habits of the women of this favoured country.

It is therefore in reference to these alone that I shall endeavour to treat the subject of England's nationality; and in order to do this with more precision, it is necessary to draw the line of observation within a narrower circle, and to describe what are the characteristics of the women of England. I ought, perhaps, in strict propriety, to say what were their characteristics; because I would justify the obtrusiveness of a work like this, by first premising that the women of England are deteriorating in their moral character, and that false notions of refinement are rendering them less influential, less useful, and less happy than they were.

In speaking of what English women were, I would not be understood to refer to what they were a century ago. Facilities in the way of mental improvement have greatly increased during this period. In connexion with moral discipline, these facilities are invaluable; but I consider the two excellencies as having been combined in the greatest perfection in the general average of women who have now attained to middle, or rather advanced age. When the cultivation of the mental faculties had so far advanced as to take precedence of the moral, by leaving no time for domestic usefulness, and the practice of personal exertion in the way of promoting general happiness, the character of the women of England assumed a different aspect, which is now beginning to tell upon society in the sickly sensibilities, the feeble frames, and the useless habits of the rising generation.

In stating this humiliating fact, I must be blind indeed to the most cheering aspect of modern society, not to perceive that there are signal instances of women who carry about with them into every sphere of domestic duty, even the most humble and obscure, the accomplishments and refinements of modern education; and who deem it rather an honour than a degradation to be permitted to add to the sum of human happiness, by diffusing the embellishments of mind and manners over the homely and familiar aspect of every-day existence.

Such, however, do not constitute the majority of the female population of Great Britain. By far the greater portion of the young ladies (for they are no longer women) of the present day, are distinguished by a morbid listlessness of mind and body, except when under the influence of stimulus, a constant pining for excitement, and an eagerness to escape from every thing like practical and individual duty. Of course, I speak of those whose minds are not under the influence of religious principle. Would that the exception could extend to all who profess to be governed by this principle!

Gentle, inoffensive, delicate, and passively amiable as many young ladies are, it seems an ungracious task to attempt to rouse them from their summer dream; and were it not that wintry days will come, and the surface of life be ruffled, and the mariner, even she who steers the smallest bark, be put upon the inquiry for what port she is really bound—were it not that the cry of utter helplessness is of no avail in rescuing from the waters of affliction, and the plea of ignorance unheard upon the far-extending and deep ocean of experience, and the question of accountability perpetually sounding, like the voice of a warning spirit, above the storms and the billows of this lower world—I would be one of the very last to call the dreamer back to a consciousness of present things. But this state of listless indifference, my sisters, must not be. You have deep responsibilities, you have urgent claims; a nation's moral wealth is in your keeping. Let us inquire then in what way it may be best preserved. Let us consider what you are, and have been, and by what peculiarities of feeling and habit you have been able to throw so much additional weight into the scale of your country's worth.

In order to speak with precision of the characteristics of any class of people, it is necessary to confine our attention as much as possible to that portion of the class where such characteristics are most prominent; and, avoiding the two extremes where circumstances not peculiar to that class are supposed to operate, to take the middle or intervening portion as a specimen of the whole.

Napoleon Buonaparte was accustomed to speak of the English nation as a "nation of shopkeepers; " and when we consider the number, the influence, and the respectability of that portion of the inhabitants who are, directly or indirectly, connected with our trade and merchandise, it does indeed appear to constitute the mass of English society, and may justly be considered as exhibiting the most striking and unequivocal proofs of what are the peculiar characteristics of the people of England. It is not therefore from the aristocracy of the land that the characteristics of English women should be taken; because the higher the rank, and the greater the facilities of communication with other countries, the more prevalent are foreign manners, and modes of thinking and acting common to that class of society in other countries. Neither is it entirely amongst the indigent and most laborious of the community, that we can with propriety look for those strong features of nationality which stamp the moral character of different nations; because the urgency of mere physical wants, and the pressure of constant and necessary labour, naturally induce a certain degree of resemblance in social feelings and domestic habits, amongst people similarly circumstanced, to whatever country they may belong.

In looking around, then, upon our "nation of shopkeepers, " we readily perceive that by dividing society into three classes, as regards what is commonly called rank, the middle class must include so vast a portion of the intelligence and moral power of the country at large, that it may not improperly be designated the pillar of our nation's strength, its base being the important class of the laborious poor, and its rich and highly ornamental capital, the ancient nobility of the land. In no other country is society thus beautifully proportioned, and England should beware of any deviation from the order and symmetry of her national column.

There never was a more short-sighted view of society, than that by which the women of our country have lately learned to look with envious eyes upon their superiors in rank, to rival their attainments, to imitate their manners, and to pine for the luxuries they enjoy; and consequently to look down with contempt upon the appliances and means of humbler happiness. The women of England were once better satisfied with that instrumentality of Divine wisdom by which they were placed in their proper sphere. They were satisfied to do with their own hands what they now leave undone, or repine that they cannot have others to do for them.

A system of philosophy was once promulgated in France, by which it was attempted to be proved that so much of the power and the cleverness of man was attributable to his hand, that, but for a slight difference in the formation of this organ in some of the inferior animals, they would have been entitled to rank in the same class with him. Whatever may be said of the capabilities of man's hand, I believe the feminine qualification of being able to use the hand willingly and well, has a great deal to do with the moral influence of woman. The personal services she is thus enabled to render, enhance her value in the domestic circle, and when such services are performed with the energy of a sound understanding, and the grace of an accomplished mind—above all, with the disinterested kindness of a generous heart—they not only dignify the performer, but confer happiness, as well as obligation. Indeed, so great is the charm of personal attentions arising spontaneously from the heart, that women of the highest rank in society, and far removed from the necessity of individual exertion, are frequently observed to adopt habits of personal kindness towards others, not only as the surest means of giving pleasure, but as a natural and grateful relief to the overflowing of their own affections.

There is a principle in woman's love, that renders it impossible for her to be satisfied without actually doing something for the object of her regard. I speak only of woman in her refined and elevated character. Vanity can satiate itself with admiration, and selfishness can feed upon services received; but woman's love is an ever-flowing and inexhaustible fountain, that must be perpetually imparting from the source of its own blessedness. It needs but slight experience to know, that the mere act of loving our fellow-crea- tures does little towards the promotion of their happiness. The human heart is not so credulous as to continue to believe in affection without practical proof. Thus the interchange of mutual kind offices begets a confidence which cannot be made to grow out of any other foundation; and while gratitude is added to the connecting link, the character on each side is strengthened by the personal energy required for the performance of every duty.

There may exist great sympathy, kindness, and benevolence of feeling, without the power of bringing any of these emotions into exercise for the benefit of others. They exist as emotions only. And thus the means, which appear to us as the most gracious and benignant of any that could have been adopted by our heavenly Father, for rousing us into necessary exertion, are permitted to die away, fruitless and unproductive, in the breast where they ought to have operated as a blessing and a means of happiness to others.

It is not uncommon to find negatively amiable individuals, who sink under a weight of indolence, and suffer from innate selfishness a gradual contraction of mind, perpetually lamenting their own inability to do good. It would be ungenerous to doubt their sincerity in these regrets. We can therefore only conclude, that the want of habits of personal usefulness has rendered them mentally imbecile, and physically inert; whereas, had the same individuals been early accustomed to bodily exertion, promptly and cheerfully performed on the spur of the moment, without waiting to question whether it was agreeable or not, the very act of exertion would have become a pleasure, and the benevolent purposes to which such exertions might be applied, a source of the highest enjoyment.

Time was when the women of England were accustomed, almost from their childhood, to the constant employment of their hands. It might be sometimes in elaborate works of fancy, now ridiculed for their want of taste, and still more frequently in household avocations, now fallen into disuse from their incompatibility with modern refinement. I cannot speak with unqualified praise of all the objects on which they bestowed their attention, but, if it were possible, I would write in characters of gold the indisputable fact, that the habits of industry and personal exertion thus acquired, gave them a strength and dignity of character, a power of usefulness, and a capability of doing good, which the higher theories of modern education fail to impart. They were in some instances less qualified for travelling on the con- tinent without an interpreter; but the women of whom I am speaking seldom went abroad. Their sphere of action was at their own firesides, and the world in which they moved was one where pleasure of the highest, purest order,

5

naturally and necessarily arises out of acts of duty faithfully performed.

Perhaps it may be necessary to be more specific in describing the class of women to which this work relates. It is, then, strictly speaking, to those who belong to that great mass of the population of England which is connected with trade and manufactures, as well as to the wives and daughters of professional men of limited incomes; or, in order to make the application more direct, to that portion of it who are restricted to the services of from one to four domestics, — who, on the one hand, enjoy the advantages of a liberal education, and, on the other, have no pretension to family rank. It is, however, impossible but that many deviations from these lines of demarcation must occur, in consequence of the great change in their pecuniary circumstances, which many families during a short period experience, and the indefinite order of rank and station in which the elegances of life are enjoyed, or its privations endured. There is also this peculiarity to be taken into account, in our view of English society, that the acquisition of wealth, with the advantages it procures, is all that is necessary for advancement to aristocratic dignity; while, on the other hand, so completely is the nation dependent upon her commercial resources, that it is no uncommon thing to see individuals who lately ranked amongst the aristocracy, suddenly driven, by the failure of some bank or some mercantile speculation, into the lowest walks of life, and compelled to mingle with the laborious poor.

These facts are strong evidence in favour of a system of conduct that would enable all women to sink gracefully, and without murmuring against providence, into a lower grade of society. It is easy to learn to enjoy, but it is not easy to learn to suffer.

Any woman of respectable education, possessing a well-regulated mind, might move with ease and dignity into a higher sphere than that to which she had been accustomed; but few women whose hands have been idle all their lives, can feel themselves compelled to do the necessary labour of a household, without a feeling of indescribable hardship, too frequently productive of a secret murmuring against the instrumentality by which she was reduced to such a lot.

It is from the class of females above described, that we naturally look for the highest tone of moral feeling, because they are at the same time removed from the pressing necessities of absolute poverty, and admitted to the intellectual privileges of the great; and thus, while they enjoy every facility in the way of acquiring knowledge, it is their still higher privilege not to be exempt from the domestic duties which call forth the best energies of the female character.

Where domestics abound, and there is a hired hand for every kindly office, it would be a work of supererogation for the mistress of the house to step forward, and assist with her own; but where domestics are few, and the individuals who compose the household are thrown upon the consideration of the mothers, wives, and daughters for their daily comfort, innumerable channels are opened for the overflow of those floods of human kindness, which it is one of the happiest and most ennobling duties of woman to administer to the weary frame, and to pour into the wounded mind.

It is perhaps the nearest approach we can make towards any thing like a definition of what is most striking in the characteristics of the women of England, to say, that the nature of their domestic circumstances is such as to invest their characters with the threefold recommendation of promptitude in action, energy of thought, and benevolence of feeling. With all the responsibilities of family comfort and social enjoyment resting upon them, and unaided by those troops of menials who throng the halls of the affluent and the great, they are kept alive to the necessity of making their own personal exertions conducive to the great end of promoting the happiness of those around them. They cannot sink into supineness, or suffer any of their daily duties to be neglected, but some beloved member of the household is made to feel the consequences, by enduring inconveniences which it is alike their pride and their pleasure to remove. The frequently recurring avocations of domestic life admit of no delay. When the performance of any kindly office has to be asked for, solicited, and re-solicited, it loses more than half its charm. It is therefore strictly in keeping with the fine tone of an elevated character, to be beforehand with expectation, and thus to show, by the most delicate yet most effectual of all human means, that the object of attention, even when unheard and unseen, has been the subject of kind and affectionate solicitude.

By experience in these apparently minute af- fairs, a woman of kindly feeling and properly disciplined mind, soon learns to regulate her actions also according to the principles of true wisdom, and hence arises that energy of thought for which the women of England are so peculiarly distinguished. Every passing event, however insignificant to the eye of the world, has its crisis, every occurrence its emergency, every cause its effect; and upon these she has to calculate with precision, or the machinery of household comfort is arrested in its movements, and thrown into disorder.

Woman, however, would but ill supply the place appointed her by providence, were she endowed with no other faculties than those of promptitude in action, and energy of thought. Valuable as these may be, they would render her but a cold and cheerless companion, without the kindly affections and tender offices that sweeten human life. It is a high privilege, then, which the women of England enjoy, to be necessarily, and by the force of circumstances, thrown upon their affections, for the rule of their conduct in daily life. "What shall I do to gratify myself—to be admired—or to vary the tenor of my existence? " are not the questions which a woman of right feeling asks on first awaking to the avocations of the day. Much more congenial to the highest attributes of woman's character, are inquiries such as these: "How shall I endeavour through this day to turn the time, the health, and the means permitted me to enjoy, to the best account? Is any one sick, I must visit their chamber without delay, and try to give their apartment an air of comfort, by arranging such things as the wearied nurse may not have thought of. Is any one about to set off on a journey, I must see that the early meal is spread, or prepare it with my own hands, in order that the servant, who was working late last night, may profit by unbroken rest. Did I fail in what was kind or considerate to any of the family yesterday; I will meet them this morning with a cordial welcome, and show, in the most delicate way I can, that I am anxious to atone for the past. Was any one exhausted by the last day's exertion, I will be an hour before them this morning, and let them see that their labour is so much in advance. Or, if nothing extraordinary occurs to claim my attention, I will meet the family with a consciousness that, being the least engaged of any member of it, I am consequently the most at liberty to devote myself to the general good of the whole, by cultivating cheerful conversation, adapting myself to the prevailing tone of feeling, and leading those who are least happy, to think and speak of what will make them more so. "

Who can believe that days, months, and years spent in a continual course of thought and action similar to this, will not produce a powerful effect upon the character; and not upon the individual who thinks, and acts, alone, but upon all to whom her influence extends?

In short, the customs of English society have so constituted women the guardians of the comfort of their homes, that, like the Vestals of old, they cannot allow the lamp they cherish to be extinguished, or to fail for want of oil, without an equal share of degradation attaching to their names.

In other countries, where the domestic lamp is voluntarily put out, in order to allow the women to resort to the opera, or the public festival, they are not only careless about their home comforts, but necessarily ignorant of the high degree of excellence to which they might be raised. In England there is a kind of science of good household management, which, if it consisted merely in keeping the house respectable in its physical character, might be left to the effectual working out of hired hands; but, happily for the women of England, there is a philosophy in this science, by which all their highest and best feelings are called into exercise. Not only must the house be neat and clean, but it must be so ordered as to suit the tastes of all, as far as may be, without annoyance or offence to any. Not only must a constant system of activity be established, but peace must be preserved, or happiness will be destroyed. Not only must elegance be called in, to adorn and beautify the whole, but strict integrity must be maintained by the minutest calculation as to lawful means, and self, and self-gratification, must be made the yielding point in every disputed case. Not only must an appearance of outward order and comfort be kept up, but around every domestic scene there must be a strong wall of confidence, which no internal suspicion can undermine, no external enemy break through.

Good household management, conducted on this plan, is indeed a science well worthy of attention. It comprises so much, as to invest it with an air of difficulty on the first view; but no woman can reasonably complain of incapability, because nature has endowed the sex with perceptions so lively and acute, that where benevolence is the impulse, and principle the foundation upon which they act, experience will soon teach them by what means they may best accomplish the end they have in view.

They will soon learn by experience, that selfish- ness produces selfishness, that indolence increases with every hour of indulgence, that what is left undone because it is difficult to-day, will be doubly difficult to-morrow; that kindness and compassion, to answer any desirable end, must one be practical, the other delicate, in its nature; that affection must be kept alive by ministering to its necessities;

and, above all, that religion must be recommended by consistency of character and conduct.

It is the strong evidence of truths like these, wrought out of their daily experience, and forced upon them as principles of action, which renders the women of England what they are, or rather were, and which fits them for becoming able instruments in the promotion of public and private good; for all must allow, that it is to the indefatigable exertions and faithful labours of women of this class, that England chiefly owes the support of some of her noblest and most benevolent institutions; while it is to their unobtrusive and untiring efforts, that the unfortunate and afflicted often are indebted for the only sympathy—the only kind attention that ever reaches their obscure abodes, or diffuses cheerfulness and comfort through the solitary chambers of suffering and sickness—the only aid that relieves the victims of penury and want—the only consolation that ever visits the desolate and degraded in their wretchedness and despair.

I acknowledge there are noble instances in the annals of English history, and perhaps never more than at the present day, of women of the highest rank devoting their time and their property to objects of benevolence; but from the very nature of their early habits and domestic circumstances, they are upon the whole less fitted for practical usefulness, than those who move within a lower sphere. I am also fully sensible of the charities which abound amongst the poor; and often have I been led to compare the actual merit of the magnificent bestowments of those who know not one comfort the less, with that of the poor man's offering and the widow's mite. Still my opinion remains the same, that in the situation of the middle class of women in England, are combined advantages in the formation of character, to which they owe much of their distinction, and their country much of her moral worth.

The true English woman, accustomed to bear about with her, her energies for daily use, her affections for daily happiness, and her delicate perceptions for hourly aids in the discovery of what is best to do or to leave undone, by this means obtains an insight into human nature, a power of adaptation, and a readiness of application of the right means to the desired end, which not only render her the most valuable friend, but the most delightful of fireside companions, because she is thus enabled to point the plainest moral, and adorn the simplest tale, with all those freshly-formed ideas which arise out of actual experience, and the contemplation of unvarnished truth.

Amongst their other characteristics, the women of England are frequently spoken of as plebeian in their manners, and cold in their affections; but their unpolished and occasionally embarrassed manner, as frequently conceals a delicacy that imparts the most refined and elevated sentiment to their familiar acts of duty and regard; and those who know them best are compelled to acknowledge, that all the noblest passions, the deepest feelings, and the highest aspirations of humanity, may be found within the brooding quiet of an English woman's heart.

There are flowers that burst upon us, and startle the eye with the splendour of their beauty; we gaze until we are dazzled, and then turn away, remembering nothing but their gorgeous hues. There are others that refresh the traveller by the sweetness they diffuse—but he has to search for the source of his delight. He finds it embedded amongst green leaves; it may be less lovely than he had anticipated, in its form and colour, but, oh! how welcome is the memory of that flower, when the evening breeze is again made fragrant with its perfume.

It is thus that the unpretending virtues of the female character force themselves upon our regard, so that the woman herself is nothing in comparison with her attributes; and we remember less the celebrated belle, than her who made us happy.

Nor is it by their frequent and faithful services alone, that English women are distinguished. The greater proportion of them were diligent and thoughtful readers. It was not with them a point of importance to devour every book that was written as soon as it came out. They were satisfied to single out the best, and, making themselves familiar with every page, conversed with the writer as with a friend, and felt that, with minds superior, but yet congenial to their own, they could make friends indeed. In this manner their solitude was cheered, their hours of labour sweetened, and their conversation rendered at once piquant and instructive. This was preserved from the technicalities of common-place by the peculiar nature of their social and mental habits. They were accustomed to think for themselves; and, deprived in some measure of access to what might be esteemed the highest authorities in matters of sentiment and taste, they drew their conclusions from reasoning, and their reasoning from actual observation. It is true, their sphere of observation was microscopic, compared with that of the individual who enjoys the means of travelling from court to court, and of mixing with the polished society of every nation; but an acute vision directed to immediate objects, whatever they may be, will often discover as much of the wonders of creation, and supply the intelligent mind with food for reflection as valuable, as that which is the result of a widely extended view, where the objects, though more numerous, are consequently less distinct.

Thus the domestic woman, moving in a comparatively limited circle, is not necessarily confined to a limited number of ideas, but can often expatiate upon subjects of mere local interest with a vigour of intellect, a freshness of feeling, and a liveliness of fancy, which create in the mind of the uninitiated stranger, a perfect longing to be admitted into the home associations from whence are derived such a world of amusement, and so unfailing a relief from the severer duties of life.

It is not from the acquisition of ideas, but from the application of them, that conversation derives its greatest charm. Thus an exceedingly well-informed talker may be indescribably tedious; while one who is comparatively ignorant, as regards mere facts, having brought to bear, upon every subject contemplated, a lively imagination combined with a sound judgment, and a memory stored, not only with dates and historical events, but with strong and clear impressions of familiar things, may rivet the attention of his hearers, and startle them, for the time, into a distinctness of impression which imparts a degree of delightful complacency both to those who listen, and to the entertainer himself.

In the exercise of this kind of tact, the women of England, when they can be induced to cast off their shyness and reserve, are peculiarly excellent, and there is consequently an originality in their humour, a firmness in their reasoning, and a tone of delicacy in their perceptions, scarcely to be found elsewhere in the same degree, and combined in the same manner; nor should it ever be forgotten, in speaking of their peculiar merits, that the freshness and the charm of their conversation is reserved for their own firesides, for moments when the wearied framed is most in need of exhi- laration, when the mind is thrown upon its own resources for the restoration of its exhausted powers, and when home associations and home affections are the balm which the wounded spirit needs.

But above all other characteristics of the women of England, the strong moral feeling pervading even their most trifling and familiar actions, ought to be mentioned as most conducive to the maintenance of that high place which they so justly claim in the society of their native land. The apparent coldness and reserve of English women ought only to be regarded as a means adopted for the preservation of their purity of mind, —an evil, if you choose to call it so, but an evil of so mild a nature, in comparison with that which it wards off, that it may with truth be said to "lean to virtue's side. "

I have said before, that the sphere of a domestic woman's observation is microscopic. She is therefore sensible of defects within that sphere, which, to a more extended vision, would be imperceptible. If she looked abroad for her happiness, she would be less disturbed by any falling off at home. If her interest and her energies were diffused through a wider range, she would be less alive to the minuter claims upon her attention. It is possible she may sometimes attach too much importance to the minutiæ of her own domestic world, especially when her mind is imperfectly cultivated and informed: but, on the other hand, there arises, from the same cause, a scrupulous exactness, a studious observance, of the means of happiness, a delicacy of perception, a purity of mind, and a dignified correctness of manner, for which the women of England are unrivalled by those of any other nation.

By a certain class of individuals, their general conduct may possibly be regarded as too prudish to be strictly in keeping with enlarged and liberal views of human life. These are such as object to find the strict principles of female action carried out towards themselves. But let every man who disputes the right foundation of this system of conduct, imagine in the place of the woman whose retiring shyness provokes his contempt, his sister or his friend; and, while he substitutes another being, similarly constituted, for himself, he will immediately perceive that the boundary-line of safety, beyond which no true friend of woman ever tempted her to pass, is drawn many degrees within that which he had marked out for his own intercourse with the female sex. Nor is it in the small and separate deviations from this strict line of pro- priety, that any great degree of culpability exists. Each individual act may be simple in itself, and almost too insignificant for remark; it is habit that stamps the character, and custom that renders common. Who then can guard too scrupulously against the first opening, the almost imperceptible chance of manners, by which the whole aspect of domestic life would be altered? And who would not rather that English women should be guarded by a wall of scruples, than allowed to degenerate into less worthy, and less efficient supporters of their country's moral worth?

Were it only in their intercourse with mixed society that English women were distinguished by this strict regard to the proprieties of life, it might with some justice fall under the ban of prudery; but happily for them, it extends to every sphere of action in which they move, discountenancing vice in every form, and investing social duty with that true moral dignity which it ought ever to possess.

I am not ignorant that this can only be consistently carried out under the influence of personal religion. I must, therefore, be understood to speak with limitations, and as comparing my own countrywomen with those of other nations—as acknowledging melancholy exceptions, and not only fervently desiring that every one professed a religion capable of leading them in a more excellent way, but that all who do profess that religion were studiously careful in these minor points. Still I do believe that the women of England are not surpassed by those of any other country for their clear perception of the right and the wrong of common and familiar things, for their reference to principle in the ordinary affairs of life, and for their united maintenance of that social order, sound integrity, and domestic peace, which constitute the foundation of all that is most valuable in the society of our native land.

Much as I have said of the influence of the domestic habits of my countrywomen, it is, after all, to the prevalence of religious instruction, and the operation of religious principle upon the heart, that the consistent maintenance of their high tone of moral character is to be attributed. Amongst families in the middle class of society in this country, those who live without regard to religion are exceptions to the general rule; while the great proportion of individuals thus circumstanced are not only accustomed to give their time and attention to religious observances, but, there is every reason to believe, are materially affected in their lives and conduct by the operation of christian principles upon their own minds. Women are said to be more easily brought under this influence than men; and we consequently see, in places of public worship, and on all occasions in which a religious object is the motive for exertion, a greater proportion of women than of men. The same proportion may possibly be observed in places of amusement, and where objects less desirable claim the attention of the public; but this ought not to render us insensible to the high privileges of our favoured country, where there is so much to interest, to please, and to instruct, in what is connected with the highest and holiest uses to which we can devote the talents committed to our trust.

Is this because women need an excuse to get out of the home?

CHAPTER II. INFLUENCE OF THE WOMEN OF ENGLAND.

IT might form a subject of interesting inquiry, how far the manifold advantages possessed by England as a country, derive their origin remotely from the cause already described; but the immediate object of the present work is to show how intimate is the connexion which exists between the women of England, and the moral character maintained by their country in the scale of nations. For a woman to undertake such a task, may at first sight appear like an act of presumption; yet when it is considered that the appropriate business of men is to direct, and expatiate upon, those expansive and important measures for which their capabilities are more peculiarly adapted, and that to women belongs the minute and particular observance of all those trifles which fill up the sum of human happiness or misery, it may surely be deemed pardonable for a woman to solicit the serious attention of her own sex, while she endeavours to prove that it is the minor morals of domestic life which give the tone to English character, and that over this sphere of duty it is her peculiar province to preside.

Aware that the word preside, used as it is here, may produce a startling effect upon the ear of man, I must endeavour to bespeak his forbearance, by assuring him, that the highest aim of the writer does not extend beyond the act of warning the women of England back to their domestic duties, in order that they may become better wives, more useful daughters, and mothers, who by their example shall bequeath a rich inheritance to those who follow in their steps.

On the other hand, I am equally aware that a work such as I am proposing to myself must be liable to the condemnation of all modern young ladies, as a homely, uninteresting book, and wholly unsuited to the present enlightened times. I must therefore endeavour also to conciliate their good will, by assuring them, that all which is most lovely, poetical, and interesting, nay, even heroic in women, derives its existence from the source I am now about to open to their view, with all the ability I am able to command; —and would it were a hundredfold, for their sakes!

The kind of encouragement I would hold out to them is, however, of a nature so widely different from the compliments to which they are too much accustomed, that I feel the difficulty existing in the present day, of stimulating a laudable ambition in the female mind, without the aid of public praise, or printed records of the actual product of their meritorious exertions. The sphere of woman's happiest and most beneficial influence is a domestic one, but it is not easy to award even to her quiet and unobtrusive virtues that meed of approbation which they really deserve, without exciting a desire to forsake the homely household duties of the family circle, to practise such as are more conspicuous, and consequently more productive of an immediate harvest of applause.

I say this with all kindness, and I desire to say it with all gentleness, to the young, the amiable, and the—vain; at the same time that my perception of the temptation to which they are exposed, enhances my value for the principle that is able to withstand it, and increases my admiration of those noble-minded women who are able to carry forward, with exemplary patience and perseverance, the public offices of benevolence, without sacrificing their home duties, and who thus prove to the world, that the perfection of female character is a combination of private and public virtue, —of domestic charity, and zeal for the temporal and eternal happiness of the whole human race.

No one can be farther than the writer of these pages from wishing to point out as objects of laudable emulation those domestic drudges, who, because of some affinity between culinary operations, and the natural tone and character of their own minds, prefer the kitchen to the drawing-room, —of their own free choice, employ their whole lives in the constant bustle of providing for mere animal appetite, and waste their ingenuity in the creation of new wants and wishes, which all their faculties again are taxed to supply. This class of individuals have, by a sad mistake in our nomenclature, been called useful, and hence, in some degree, may arise the unpopular reception which this valuable word is apt to meet with in female society.

It does not require much consideration to perceive that these are not the women to give a high moral tone to the national character of England; yet so entirely do human actions derive their digity or their meanness from the motives by which they are prompted, that it is no violation of truth to say, the most servile drudgery may be ennobled by the self-sacrifice, the patience, the cheerful submission to duty, with which it is performed. Thus a high-minded and intellectual woman is never more truly great than when willingly and judiciously performing kind offices for the sick; and much as may be said, and said justly, in praise of the public virtues of women, the voice of nature is so powerful in every human heart, that could the question of superiority on these two points be universally proposed, a response would be heard throughout the world, in favour of woman in her private and domestic character.

Nor would the higher and more expansive powers of usefulness with which women are endowed, suffer from want of exercise, did they devote themselves assiduously to their domestic duties. I am rather inclined to think they would receive additional vigour from the healthy tone of their own minds, and the leisure and liberty afforded by the systematic regularity of their household affairs. Time would never hang heavily on their hands, but each moment being husbanded with care, and every agent acting under their influence being properly chosen and instructed, they would find ample opportunity to go forth on errands of mercy, secure that in their absence, the machinery they had set in motion would still continue to work, and to work well.

But if, on the other hand, all was confusion and neglect at home— filial appeals unanswered—domestic comforts uncalculated— husbands, sons, and brothers, referred to servants for all the little offices of social kindness, in order that the ladies of the family might hurry away at the appointed time to some committee-room, scientific lecture, or public assembly; however laudable the object for which they met, there would be sufficient cause why their cheeks should be mantled with the blush of burning shame when they heard the women of England and their virtues spoken of in that high tone of approbation and applause, which those who aspire only to be about their Master's business will feel little pleasure in listening to, and which those whose charity has not begun at home, ought never to appropriate to themselves.

It is a widely mistaken notion to suppose that the sphere of usefulness recommended here, is a humiliating and degraded one. As if the earth that fosters and nourishes in its lovely bosom the roots of all the plants and trees which ornament the garden of the world, feeding them from her secret storehouse with supplies that never fail, were less important, in the economy of vegetation, than the sun that brings to light their verdure and their flowers, or the genial atmosphere that perfects their growth, and diffuses their perfume abroad upon the earth. To carry out the simile still farther, it is but just to give the preference to that element which, in the absence of all other favouring circumstances, withholds not its support; but when the sun is shrouded, and the showers forget to fall, and blighting winds go forth, and the hand of culture is withdrawn, still opens out its hidden fountains, and yields up its resources, to invigorate, to cherish, and sustain.

It would be an easy and a grateful task, thus, by metaphor and illustration, to prove the various excellencies and amiable peculiarities of woman, did not the utility of the present work demand a more minute and homely detail of that which constitutes her practical and individual duty. It is too much the custom with writers, to speak in these general terms of the loveliness of the female character; as if woman were some fragrant flower, created only to bloom, and exhale in sweets: when perhaps these very writers are themselves most strict in requiring that the domestic drudgery of their own households should each day be faithfully filled up. How much more generous, just, and noble it would be to deal fairly by woman in these matters, and to tell her that to be individully, what she is praised for being in general, it is necessary for her to lay aside all her natural caprice, her love of self-indulgence, her vanity, her indolence—in short, her very self—and assuming a new nature, which nothing less than watchfulness and prayer can enable her constantly to maintain, to spend her mental and moral capabilities in devising means for promoting the happiness of others, while her own derives a remote and secondary existence from theirs.

If an admiration almost unbounded for the perfection of female character, with a sisterly participation in all the errors and weaknesses to which she is liable, and a profound sympathy with all that she is necessarily compelled to feel and suffer, are qualifications for the task I have undertaken, these certainly are points on which I yield to none; but at the same time that I do my feeble best, I must deeply regret that so few are the voices lifted up in her defence against the dangerous influence of popular applause, and the still more dangerous tendency of modern habits, and modern education. Perhaps it is not to be expected that those who write most powerfully, should most clearly perceive the influence of the one, or the tendency of the other; because the very strength and consistency of their own minds must in some measure exempt them from participation in either. While, therefore, in the art of reasoning, a writer like myself must be painfully sensible of her own deficiency;

in sympathy of feeling, she is perhaps the better qualified to address the weakest of her sex.

With such, it is a favourite plea, brought forward in extenuation of their own uselessness, that they have no influence—that they are not leading women—that society takes no note of them; —forgetting, while they shelter themselves beneath these indolent excuses, that the very feather on the stream may serve to warn the doubtful mariner of the rapid and fatal current by which his bark might be hurried to destruction. It is, moreover, from amongst this class that wives are more frequently chosen; for there is a peculiarity in men—I would fain call it benevolence—which inclines them to offer the benefit of their protection to the most helpless and dependent of the female sex; and therefore it is upon this class that the duty of training up the young most frequently devolves; not certainly upon the naturally imbecile, but upon the uncalculating creatures whose non-exercise of their own mental and moral facul- ties renders them not only willing to be led through the experience of life, but thankful to be relieved from the responsibility of thinking and acting for themselves.

It is an important consideration, that from such women as these, myriads of immortal beings derive that early bias of character, which under Providence decides their fate, not only in this world, but in the world to come. And yet they flutter on, and say they have no influence—they do not aspire to be leading women—they are in society but as grains of sand on the sea-shore. Would they but pause one moment to ask how will this plea avail them, when, as daughters without gratitude, friends without good faith, wives without consideration, and mothers without piety, they stand before the bar of judgment, to render an account of the talents committed to their trust! Have they not parents, to whom they might study to repay the debt of care and kindness accumulated in their clildhood? —perhaps to whom they might overpay this debt, by assisting to remove such obstacles as apparently intercept the line of duty, and by endeavouring to alleviate the perplexing cares which too often obscure the path of life? Have they not their young friendships, for those sunny hours when the heart expands itself in the genial atmosphere of mutual love, and shrinks not from revealing its very weaknesses and errors; so that a faithful hand has but to touch its tender chords, and conscience is awakened, and then instruction may be poured in, and medicine may be administered, and the messenger of peace, with healing on his wings, may be invited to come in, and make that heart his home? Have they not known the secrets of some faithful bosom laid bare before them in a deeper and yet more confiding attachment, when, however insignificant they might be to the world in general, they held an influence almost unbounded over one human being, and could pour in, for the bane or the blessing of that bosom, according to the fountain from whence their own was supplied, either draughts of bitterness, or floods of light? Have they not bound themselves by a sacred and enduring bond, to be to one fellow-traveller along the path of life, a companion on his journey, and, as far as ability might be granted them, a guide and a help in the doubts and the difficulties of his way? Under these urgent and serious responsibilities, have they not been appealed to, both in words and in looks, and in the silent language of the heart, for that promised help? And how has the appeal been answered? Above all, have they not, many of them, had the feeble steps of infancy committed to their care—the pure unsullied page of childhood presented to them for its first and most durable inscription? —and what have they written there? It is vain to plead their inability, and say they knew not what to write, and therefore left the tablet untouched, or sent away the vacant page to be filled up by other hands. Time will prove to them they have written, if not by any direct instrumentality, by their example, their conversation, and the natural influence of mind on mind. Experience will prove to them they have written; and the transcript of what they have written will be treasured up, either for or against them, amongst the awful records of eternity.

It is therefore not only false in reasoning, but wrong in principle, for women to assert, as they not unfrequently do with a degree of puerile satisfaction, that they have no influence. An influence fraught either with good or evil, they must have; and though the one may be above their ambition, and the other beyond their fears, by neglecting to obtain an influence which shall be beneficial to society, they necessarily assume a bad one: just in the same proportion as their selfishness, indolence, or vacuity of mind, render them in youth an easy prey to every species of unamiable tem- per, in middle age the melancholy victims of mental disease, and, long before the curtain of death conceals their follies from the world, a burden and a bane to society at large.

A superficial observer might rank with this class many of those exemplary women, who pass to and fro upon the earth with noisless step, whose names are never heard, and who, even in society, if they attempt to speak, have scarcely the ability to command an attentive audience. Yet amongst this unpretending class are found striking and noble instances of women, who, apparently feeble and insignificant, when called into action by pressing and peculiar circumstances, can accomplish great and glorious purposes, supported and carried forward by that most valuable of all faculties—moral power. And just in proportion as women cultivate this faculty (under the blessing of heaven) independently of all personal attractions, and unaccompanied by any high attainments in learning or art, is their influence over their fellow-creatures, and consequently their power of doing good.

It is not to be persumed that women possesss more moral power than men; but happily for them, such are their early impressions, associations, and general position in the world, that their moral feelings are less liable to be impaired by the pecu- niary objects which too often constitute the chief end of man, and which, even under the limitations of better principle, necessarily engage a large portion of his thoughts. There are many humble-minded women, not remarkable for any particular intellectual endowments, who yet possess so clear a sense of the right and wrong of individual actions, as to be of essential service in aiding the judgments of their husbands, brothers, or sons, in those intricate affairs in which it is sometimes difficult to dissever worldly wisdom from religious duty.

To men belongs the potent—(I had almost said the omnipotent) consideration of worldly aggrandisement; and it is constantly misleading their steps, closing their ears against the voice of conscience, and beguiling them with the promise of peace, where peace was never found. Long before the boy has learned to exult in the dignity of the man, his mind has become familiarized to the habit of investing with supreme importance, all considerations relating to the acquisition of wealth. He hears on the Sabbath, and on stated occasions, when men meet for that especial purpose, of a God to be worshipped, a Saviour to be trusted in, and a holy law to be observed; but he sees before him, every day and every hour, a strife, which is nothing less than deadly to the highest impulses of the soul, after another god—the mammon of unrighteousness—the moloch of this world; and believing rather what men do, than what they preach, he learns too soon to mingle with the living mass, and to unite his labours with theirs. To unite? Alas! there is no union in the great field of action in which he is engaged; but envy, and hatred, and opposition, to the close of the day—every man's hand against his brother, and each struggling to exalt himself, not merely by trampling upon his fallen foe, but by usurping the place of his weaker brother, who faints by his side, from not having brought an equal portion of strength into the conflict, and who is consequently borne down by numbers, hurried over, and forgotten.

This may be an extreme, but it is scarcely an exaggerated picture of the engagements of men of business in the present day. And surely they now need more than ever all the assistance which Providence has kindly provided, to win them away from this warfare, to remind them that they are hastening on towards a world into which none of the treasures they are amassing can be admitted; and, next to those holier influences which operate through the medium of revelation, or through the mysterious instrumentality of Divine love, I have little hesitation in saying, that the society of woman in her highest moral capacity, is best calculated to effect this purpose.

How often has man returned to his home with a mind confused by the many voices, which in the mart, the exchange, or the public assembly, have addressed themselves to his inborn selfishness, or his worldly pride; and while his integrity was shaken, and his resolution gave way beneath the pressure of apparent necessity, or the insidious pretences of expediency, he has stood corrected before the clear eye of woman, as it looked directly to the naked truth, and detected the lurking evil of the specious act he was about to commit. Nay, so potent may have become this secret influence, that he may have borne it about with him like a kind of second conscience, for mental reference, and spiritual counsel, in moments of trial; and when the snares of the world were around him, and temptations from within and without have bribed over the witness in his own bosom, he has thought of the humble monitress who sat alone, guarding the fireside comforts of his distant home; and the remembrance of her character, clothed in moral beauty, has scattered the clouds before his mental vision, and sent him back to that beloved home, a wiser and a better man.

The women of England, possessing the grand privilege of being better instructed than those of any other country, in the minutiæ of domestic comfort, have obtained a degree of importance in society far beyond what their unobtrusive virtues would appear to claim. The long-established customs of their country have placed in their hands the high and holy duty of cherishing and protecting the minor morals of life, from whence springs all that is elevated in purpose, and glorious in action. The sphere of their direct personal influence is central, and consequently small; but its extreme operations are as widely extended as the range of human feeling. They may be less striking in society than some of the women of other countries, and may feel themselves, on brilliant and stirring occasions, as simple, rude, and unsophisticated in the popular science of excitement; but as far as the noble daring of Britain has sent forth her adventurous sons, and that is to every point of danger on the habitable globe, they have borne along with them a generosity, a disinterestedness, and a moral courage, derived in so small measure from the female influence of their native country.

It is a fact well worthy of our most serious attention, and one which bears immediately upon the subject under consideration, that the present state of our national affairs is such as to indicate that the influence of woman in counteracting the growing evils of society is about to be more needed than ever.

In our imperfect state of being, we seldom attain any great or national good without its accompaniment of evil; and every improvement proposed for the general weal, has, upon some individual, or some class of individuals, an effect which it requires a fresh exercise of energy and principle to guard against. Thus the great facilities of communication, not only throughout our own country, but with distant parts of the world, are rousing men of every description to tenfold exertion in the field of competition in which they are engaged; so that their whole being is becoming swallowed up in efforts and calculations relating to their pecuniary success. If to grow tardy or indifferent in the race were only to lose the goal, many would be glad to pause; but such is the nature of commerce and trade, as at present carried on in this country, that to slacken in exertion, is altogether to fail. I would fain hope and believe of my countrymen, that many of the rational and enlightened would now be willing to reap smaller gains, if by so doing they could enjoy more leisure. But a business only half attended to, soon ceases to be a business at all; and the man of enlightened understanding, who neglects his, for the sake of hours of leisure, must be content to spend them in the debtor's department of a jail.

Thus, it is not with single individuals that the blame can be made to rest. The fault is in the system; and happy will it be for thousands of immortal souls, when this system shall correct itself. In the mean time, may it not be said to be the especial duty of women to look around them, and see in what way they can counteract this evil, by calling back the attention of man to those sunnier spots in his existence, by which the growth of his moral feelings have been encouraged, and his heart improved?

We cannot believe of the fathers who watched over our childhood, of the husbands who shared our intellectual pursuits, of the brothers who went hand in hand with us in our love of poetry and nature, that they are all gone over to the side of mammon, that there does not lurk in some corner of their hearts a secret longing to return; yet every morning brings the same hurried and indifferent parting, every evening the same jaded, speechless, welcomeless return—until we almost fail to recognize the man, in the machine.

English homes have been much boasted of by English people, both at home and abroad. What would a foreigner think of those neat, and sometimes elegant residences, which form a circle of comparative gentility around our cities and our trading towns? What would he think, when told that the fathers of those families have not time to see their children, except on the Sabbath-day? and that the mothers, impatient, and anxious to consult them about some of their domestic plans, have to wait, perhaps for days, before they can find them for five minutes disengaged, either from actual exertion, or from that sleep which necessarily steals upon them immediately after the over-excitement of the day has permitted them a moment of repose.

And these are rational, intellectual, accountable, and immortal beings, undergoing a course of discipline by which they are to be fitted for eternal existence! What woman can look on without asking—"Is there nothing I can do, to call them back? " Surely there is; but it never can be done by the cultivation of those faculties which contribute only to selfish gratification. Since her society is shared for so short a time, she must endeavour to make those moments more rich in blessing; and since her influence is limited to so small a range of immediate operation, it should be rendered so potent as to mingle with the whole existence of those she loves.

Will an increase of intellectual attainments, or a higher style of accomplishments, effect this purpose? Will the common-place frivolities of morning calls, or an interminable range of superficial reading, enable them to assist their brothers, their husbands, or their sons in becoming happier and better men?

No: let the aspect of society be what it may, man is a social being, and beneath the hard surface he puts on, to fit him for the wear and tear of every day, he has a heart as true to the kindly affections of our nature, as that of woman—as true, though not as suddenly awakened to every pressing call. He has therefore need of all her sisterly services, and, under the pressure of the present times, he needs them more than ever, to foster in his nature, and establish in his character, that higher tone of feeling, without which he can enjoy nothing beyond a kind of animal existence—but with which, he may faithfully pursue the necessary avocations of the day, and keep as it were a separate soul for his family, his social duty, and his God.

There is another point of consideration by which this necessity for a higher degree of female influence is greatly increased, and it is one which comprises much that is interesting to those who aspire to be the supporters of their country's worth. The British throne being now graced by a female sovereign, the auspicious promise of whose early years seems to form a new era in the annals of our nation, and to inspire with brighter hopes and firmer confidence the patriot bosoms of her expectant people; it is surely not a time for the female part of the community to fall away from the high standard of moral excellence, to which they have been accustomed to look, in the formation of their domestic habits. Rather let them show forth the benefits arising from their more enlightened systems of education, by proving to their youthful sovereign, that whatever plan she may think it right to sanction for the moral advancement of her subjects, and the promotion of their true interests as an intelligent and happy people, will be welcomed by every female heart throughout her realm, and faithfully supported in every British home by the female influence prevailing there.

It will be the business of the writer, through the whole of the succeeding pages of this work, to endeavour to point out, how the women of England may render this important service, not only to the members of their own households, but to the community at large: and if I fail in arousing them to bring as with one mind, their united powers to stem the popular torrent now threatening to undermine the strong foundation of England's moral worth, it will not be for want of earnestness in the cause, but because I am not endowed with talent equal to the task.

CHAPTER III. MODERN EDUCATION.

IN writing on the subject of modern education, I cannot help entertaining a fear lest some remarks I may in candour feel constrained to make, should be construed into disrespect towards that truly praiseworthy and laborious portion of the community, employed in conducting this education, and pursuing, with laudable endeavours, what is generally believed to be the best method of training up the young women of the present day. Such, however, is the real state of my own sentiments, that I have long been accustomed to consider this class of individuals as not only entitled to the highest pecuniary consideration, but equally so to the first place in society, to the gratitude of their fellow-creatures, and to the respect of mankind in general, who, both as individuals, and as a com- munity, are deeply indebted to them for their indefatigable and often ill-requited services.

A woman of cultivated understanding and correct religious principle, when engaged in the responsible task of educating the rising generation, in reality fills one of the most responsible stations to which a human being can aspire; and nothing can more clearly indicate a low state of public morals than the vulgar disrespect and parsimonious remuneration with which the agents employed in education are sometimes requited.

It is with what is taught, not with those who teach, that I am daring enough to find fault. It may be that I am taking an unenlightened and prejudiced view of the subject; yet, such is the strong conviction of my own mind, that I cannot rest without attempting to prove that the present education of the women of England does not fit them for faithfully performing the duties which devolve upon them immediately after their leaving school, and throughout the whole of their after lives—does not convert them from helpless children, into such characters as all women must be, in order to be either esteemed or admired.

Nor are their teachers accountable for this. It is the fashion of the day—it is the ambition of the times, that all people should, as far as possible, learn all things of which the human intellect takes cognizance; and what would be the consternation of parents whose daughter should return home to them from school unskilled in modern accomplishments, —to whom her governess should say, "It is true I have been unable to make your child a proficient either in French or Latin, nor is she very apt at the use of the globes, but she has been pre-eminent amongst my scholars for her freedom from selfishness, and she possesses a nobility of feeling that will never allow her to be the victim of meanness, or the slave of grovelling desires. "

In order to ascertain what kind of education is most effective in making woman what she ought to be, the best method is to inquire into the character, station, and peculiar duties of woman throughout the largest portion of her earthly career; and then ask, for what she is most valued, admired, and beloved?

In answer to this, I have little hesitation in saying, —For her disinterested kindness. Look at all the heroines, whether of romance or reality—at all the female characters that are held up to universal admiration—at all who have gone down to honoured graves, amongst the tears and the lamentations of their survivors. Have these been the learned, the accomplished women; the women who could speak many languages, who could solve problems, and elucidate systems of philosophy? No: or if they have, they have also been women who were dignified with the majesty of moral greatness—women who regarded not themselves, their own feebleness, or their own susceptibility of pain, but who, endued with an almost superhuman energy, could trample under-foot every impediment that intervened between them and the accomplishment of some great object upon which their hopes were fixed, while that object was wholly unconnected with their own personal exaltation or enjoyment, and related only to some beloved object, whose suffering was their sorrow, whose good their gain.

Woman, with all her accumulation of minute disquietudes, her weakness, and her sensibility, is but a meagre item in the catalogue of humanity but, roused by a sufficient motive to forget all these, or, rather, continually forgetting them because she has other and nobler thoughts to occupy her mind, woman is truly and majestically great.

Never yet, however, was woman great, because she had great acquirements; nor can she ever be great in herself—personally, and without instrumentality—as an object, not an agent.

From the beginning to the end of school education, the improvement of self, so far as relates to intellectual attainments, is made the rule and the motive of all that is done. Rewards are appointed and portioned out for what has been learned, not what has been imparted. To gain, is the universal order of the establishment; and those who have heaped together the greatest sum of knowledge are usually regarded as the most meritorious. Excellent discourses may be delivered by the preceptress upon the christian duties of benevolence and disinterested love; but the whole system is one of pure selfishness, fed by accumulation, and rewarded by applause. To be at the head of the class to gain the ticket or the prize, are the points of universal ambition; and few individuals, amongst the community of aspirants, are taught to look forward with a rational presentiment to that future, when their merit will be to give the place of honour to others, and their happiness to give it to those who are more worthy than themselves.

We will not assert that no one entertains such thoughts; for there is a voice in woman's heart too strong for education—a principle which the march of intellect is unable to overthrow.

Retiring from the emulous throng, we sometimes find a little, despised, neglected girl, who has won no prize, obtained no smile of approbation from her superiors. She is a dull girl, who learns slowly, and cannot be taught so as to keep up with the rest without incalculable pains. The fact is, she has no great wish to keep up with them: she only wants to be loved and trusted by her teachers; and oh! how does she wish, with tears, and almost with prayers, that they would love and trust her, and give her credit for doing her best. Beyond this she is indifferent; she has no motive but that of pleasing others, for trying to be clever; and she is quite satisfied that her friend, the most ambitious girl in the school, should obtain all the honours without her competition. Indeed, she feels as though it scarcely would be delicate, scarcely kind in her, to try so much to advance before her friend; and she gently falls back, is reproved for her neglect, and, finally, despised.

I knew a girl who was one of the best grammarians in a large school, whose friend was peculiarly defective in that particular branch of learning. Once every year the order of the class was reversed, the girl who held the highest place exchanging situations with the lowest, and thus affording all an equal chance of obtaining honours. The usual order of the class was soon restored, except that the good grammarian was always expected by her friend to whisper in her ear a suitable answer to every question proposed; and as this girl necessarily retrograded to the place to which her own ignorance entitled her, her friend felt bound by affection and kindness to relieve her distress every time the alarming question came to her turn She consequently remained the lowest in the class until the time of her leaving the school, often subjected to the reproofs of her teachers, and fully alive to her humiliating situation, but never once turning a deaf ear to her friend, or refusing to assist her in her difficulties.

In the schools of the ancients, an act of patient disinterestedness like this, would have met with encouragement and reward; in the school where it took place, it was well for both parties that it was never known.

In making these and similar remarks, I am aware that I may bring upon myself the charge of wishing to exclude from our schools all intellectual attainments whatever; for how, it will be asked, can learning be acquired without emulation, and without rewards for the diligent, and punishments for the idle?

So far, however, from wishing to cast a shade of disrespect over such attainments, I am decidedly of opinion that no human being can know too much, so long as the sphere of knowledge does not extend to what is positively evil. I am also of opinion that there is scarcely any department of art or science, still less of mental application, which is not calculated to strengthen and improve the mind; but at the same time I regard the improvement of the heart of so much greater consequence, that if time and opportunity should fail for both, I would strenuously recommend that women should be sent home from school with fewer accomplishments, and more of the will and the power to perform the various duties necessarily devolving upon them.

Again, I am reminded of the serious and important fact, that religion alone can improve the heart; and to this statement no one can field assent with more reverential belief in its truth than myself. I acknowledge, also, for I know it to be a highly creditable fact, that a large proportion of the meritorious individuals who take upon themselves the arduous task of training up the young, are conscientiously engaged in giving to religious instruction that place which it ought unquestionably to hold in every christian school. But I would ask, is instruction all that is wanted for instilling into the minds of the rising generation the benign principles of christian faith and practice?

It is not thought enough to instruct the young sculptor in the rules of his art, to charge his memory with the names of those who have excelled in it, and, with the principles they have laid down for the guidance of others. —No: he must work with his own hand; and long before that hand, and the mind by which it is influenced, have attained maturity, he must have learned to mould the pliant clay, and have thus become familiar with the practice of his art.

And shall this universally acknowledged system of instruction, for which we are indebted for all that is excellent in art and admirable in science, be neglected in the education of the young Christian alone? Shall he be taught the bare theory of his religion, and left to work out its practice as he can? Shall he be instructed in what he is to believe, and not assisted in doing also the will of his heavenly Father?

We all know that it is not easy to practise even the simplest rule of right, when we have not been accustomed to do so; and the longer we are before we begin to regulate our conduct by the precepts of religion, the more difficult it will be to acquire such habits as are calculated to adorn and show forth the purity and excellence of its principles.

There is one important difference between the acquisition of knowledge, and the acquisition of good habits, which of itself ought to be sufficient to ensure a greater degree of attention to the latter. When the little pupil first begins her education, her mind is a total blank, as far as relates to the different branches of study into which she is about to be introduced, and there is consequently nothing to oppose. She is not prepossessed in favour of any false system of arithmetic, grammar, or geography, and the ideas presented to her on these subjects are consequently willingly received, and adopted as her own.

How different is the moral state of the uninstructed child! Selfishness coeval with her existence has attained an alarming growth; and all the other passions and propensities inherent in her nature, taking their natural course, have strengthened with her advance towards maturity, and are ready to assume an aspect too formidable to afford any prospect of their being easily brought into subjection.

Yet, notwithstanding this difference, the whole machinery of education is brought to bear upon the intellectual part of her nature, and her moral feelings are left to the training of the play-ground, where personal influence rather than right feeling, too frequently decides her disputes, and places her either high or low in the ranks of her companions.

It is true, she is very seriously and properly corrected when convicted of having done wrong, and an admirable system of morals is promulgated in the school; but the subject I would complain of is, that no means have yet been adopted for making the practice of this system the object of highest importance in our schools. No adequate means have been adopted for testing the generosity, the high-mindedness, the integrity of the children who pursue their education at school, until they leave it at the age of sixteen, when their moral faculties, either for good or for evil, must have attained considerable growth.

Let us single out from any particular seminary a child who has been there from the years of ten to fifteen, and reckon, if it can be reckoned, the pains that have been spent in making that child a proficient in Latin. Have the same pains been spent in making her disinterestedly kind? And yet what man is there in existence who would not rather his wife should be free from selfishness, than be able to read Virgil without the use of a dictionary.

There is no reason, however, why both these desirable ends should not be aimed at, and as the child progresses in self-denial, forbearance, generosity, and disinterested kindness, it might be her reward to advance in the acquisition of languages, or of whatever accomplishments it might be thought most desirable for her to attain. If I am told there would not be time for all the discipline requisite for the practice of morals; I ask in reply, how much do most young ladies learn at school, for which they never find any use in after life, and for which, it is not probable from their circumstances that they ever should. Let the hours spent upon music by those who have no ear—upon drawing, by those who might almost be said to have no eye—upon languages, by those who never afterwards speak any other than their mother-tongue—be added together year after year; and an aggregate of wasted time will present itself, sufficient to alarm those who are sensible of its value, and of the awful responsibility of using it aright.

It is impossible that the teachers or even the parents themselves should always know the future destiny of the child; but there is an appropriate sphere for women to move in, from which those of the middle class in England seldom deviate very widely. This sphere has duties and occupations of its own, from which no woman can shrink without culpability and disgrace; and the question is, are women prepared for these duties and occupations by what they learn at school?

For my own part, I know not how education deserves the name, if it does not prepare the individual whom it influences, for filling her appointed station in the best possible manner. What, for instance, should we think of a school for sailors, in which nothing was taught but the fine arts; or for musicians, in which the students were only instructed in the theory of sound?

With regard of the women of England, I have already ventured to assert that the quality for which, above all others, they are esteemed and valued, is their disinterested kindness. A selfish woman may not improperly be regarded as a monster, especially in that sphere of life, where there is a constant demand made upon her services. But how are women taught at school to forget themselves, and to cultivate that high tone of generous feeling to which the world is so much indebted for the hope and the joy, the peace and the consolation, which the influence and companionship of woman is able to diffuse throughout its very deserts, visiting, as with blessed sun- shine, the abodes of the wretched and the poor, and sharing cheerfully the lot of the afflicted.

In what school, or under what system of modern education, can it be said that the chief aim of the teachers, the object to which their laborious exertions are mainly directed, is to correct the evil of selfishness in the hearts of their pupils? Improved methods of charging and surcharging the memory are eagerly sought out, and pursued, at any cost of time and patience, if not of health itself; but who ever thinks of establishing a selfish class amongst the girls of her establishment, or of awarding the honours and distinctions of the school to such as have exhibited the most meritorious instances of self-denial for the benefit of others.

It may be objected to this plan, that virtue ought to be its own reward, and that honours and rewards adjudged to the most meritorious in a moral point of view, would be likely to induce a degree of self-complacency wholly inconsistent with christian meekness. I am aware that, in our imperfect state, no plan can be laid down for the promotion of good, with which evil will not be liable to mix. All I contend for is, that the same system of discipline, with the same end in view, should be begun and carried on at school, as that to which the scholar will necessarily be subjected in after life; and that throughout the training of her early years, the same standard of merit should be adopted, as she will find herself compelled to look up to, when released from that training, and sent forth into the world to think and act for herself.

At school it has been the business of every day to raise herself above her companions by attainments greater than theirs; in after life it will be the business of every day to give place to others, to think of their happiness, and to make sacrifices of her own to promote it. If such acts of self-denial, when practised at school, should endanger the equanimity of her mind by the approbation they obtain, what will they do in the world she is about to enter, where the unanimous opinion of mankind, both in this, and in past ages, is in their favour, and where she must perpetually hear woman spoken of in terms of the highest commendation, not for her learning, but for her disinterested kindness, her earnest zeal in promoting the happiness of her fellow-creatures, and the patience and forbearance with which she studies to mitigate affliction and relieve distress?

Would it not be safer, then, to begin at a very early age to make the practice of these virtues the chief object of their lives, guarding at the same time against any self-complacency that might attach to the performance of them, by keeping always before their view, higher and nobler instances of virtue in others; and especially by a strict and constant reference to the utter worthlessness of all human merit, in comparison with the mercy and forgiveness that must ever impose a debt of gratitude upon our own souls?

Taking into consideration the various excellencies and peculiarities of woman, I am inclined to think that the sphere which of all others admits of the highest developement of her character, is the chamber of sickness; and how frequently and mournfully familiar are the scenes in which she is thus called to act and feel, let the private history of every family declare.

There is but a very small proportion of the daughters of farmers, manufacturers, and tradespeople, in England, who are ever called upon for their Latin, their Italian, or even for their French; but all women in this sphere of life are liable to be called upon to visit and care for the sick; and if in the hour of weakness and of suffering, they prove to be unacquainted with any probable means of alleviation, and wholly ignorant of the most judicious and suitable mode of offering relief and consolation, they are indeed deficient in one of the highest attainments in the way of usefulness, to which a woman can aspire.

To obviate the serious difficulties which many women experience from this cause, I would propose, as a substitute for some useless accomplishments, that English girls should be made acquainted with the most striking phenomena of some of the familiar, and frequently recurring maladies to which the human frame is liable, with the most approved methods of treatment. And by cultivating this knowledge so far as relates to general principles, I have little doubt but it might be made an interesting and highly useful branch of education.

I am far from wishing them to interfere with the province of the physician. The more they know, the less likely they will be to do this. The office of a judicious nurse is all I would recommend them to aspire to; and to the same department of instruction should be added the whole science of that delicate and difficult cookery which forms so important a part of the attendant's duty.

Nor let these observations call forth a smile upon the rosy lips that are yet unparched by fever, untainted by consumption. Fair reader, there have been those who would have given at the moment almost half their worldly wealth, to have been able to provide a palatable morsel for a beloved sufferer; who have met the inquiring eye, that asked for it knew not what, and that expressed by its anxious look an almost childish longing for what they were unable to supply, not because the means were denied, but simply because they were too ignorant of the nature and necessities of illness to form any practical idea of what would be most suitable and most approved. Perhaps, in their well-meant officiousness, they have mentioned the only thing they were acquainted with, and that was just the most repulsive. What then have they done? —Allowed the faint and feeble sufferer to go pining on, wishing it had been her lot to fall under the care of any other nurse.

How invaluable at such a time is the almost endless catalogue of good and suitable preparations with which the really clever woman is supplied, any one of which she is able to prepare with her own hands; choosing, with the skill of the doctor, what is best adapted for the occasion, and converting diet into medicine of the most agreeable description, which she brings silently into the sick-room without previous mention, and thus exhilarates the spirits of the patient by an agreeable surprise.

It is customary with young ladies of the present day to think that nurses and hired attendants ought to do these things; and well and faithfully they sometimes do them, to the shame of those connected by nearer ties. But are they ignorant that a hired hand can never impart such sweetness to a cordial as a hand beloved; and that the most delicious and most effectual means of proving the strength of their affection is to choose to do, what might by possibility have been accomplished by another?

When we meet in society with that speechless inanimate, ignorant, and useless being called "a young lady just come from school, " it is thought a sufficient apology for all her deficiencies, that she has, poor thing! but just come home from school. Thus implying that nothing in the way of domestic usefulness, social intercourse, or adaptation to circumstances, can be expected from her until she has had time to learn it.

If, during the four or five years spent at school, she had been establishing herself upon the foundation of her future character, and learning to practise what would afterwards be the business of her life, she would, when her education was considered as complete, be in the highest possible state of perfection which her nature, at that season of life, would admit of. This is what she ought to be. I need not advert to what she is. The case is too pitiful to justify any farther description. The popular and familiar remark, "Poor thing! she has just come home from school; what can you expect? " is the best commentary I can offer.

There is another point of difference between the training of the intellect, and that of the moral feelings, of more serious importance than any we have yet considered.

We all know that the occupation of teaching, as it relates to the common branches of instruction, is one of such herculean labour, that few persons are found equal to it for any protracted length of time; and even with such, it is necessary that they should bend their minds to it with a determined effort, and make each day a renewal of that effort, not to be baffled by difficulties, nor defeated by want of success. We all know, too, what it is to the learner to be dragged on day by day through the dull routine of exercises, in which she feels no particular interest, except what arises from getting in advance of her fellows, obtaining a prize, or suffering a punishment. We all can remember the atmosphere of the school-room, so uncongenial to the fresh and buoyant spirits of youth—the clatter of slates, the dull point of the pencil, and the white cloud where the wrong figure, the figure that would prove the incorrectness of the whole, had so often been rubbed out. To say nothing of the morning lessons, before the dust from the desks and the floor had been put in motion, we all can remember the afternoon sensations with which we took our places, perhaps between companions the most unloved by us of any in the school; and how, while the summer's sun was shining in through the high windows, we pored with aching head over some dry dull words, that would not transmit themselves to the tablet of our memories, though repeated with indefatigable industry, repeated until they seemed to have no identity, no distinctness, but were mingled with the universal hum and buzz of the close, heated room; where the heart, if it did not forget itself to stone, at least forgot itself to sleep, and lost all power of feeling anything but weariness, and occasional pining for relief. Class after class were then called up from this hot-bed of intellect. The tones of the teacher's voice, though not always the most musical, might easily have been pricked down in notes, they were so uniform in their cadences of interrogation, rejection, and reproof. These, blending with the slow, dull answers of the scholars, and occasionally the quick guess of one ambitious to attain the highest place, all mingled with the general monotony, and increased the stupor that weighed down every eye, and deadened every pulse.

There are, unquestionably, quick children, who may easily be made fond of learning, if judiciously treated; and it no doubt happens to all, that there are portions of their daily duty not absolutely disagreeable; but that weariness is the prevalent sensation both with the teachers and the taught, is a fact that few will attempt to deny; nor is it a libel upon individuals thus engaged, or upon human nature in general, that it should be so. We are so constituted that we cannot spend all our time in the exercise of our intellect, without absolute pain, especially while young; and when, in after life, we rise with exhausted patience from three hours of writing or reading we cannot look back with wonder that at school we suffered severely from the labour of six.

It is not my province to describe how much the bodily constitution is impaired by this incessant application to study. Philanthropical means are devised for relieving the young student as much as possible, by varying the subjects of attention, and allowing short intervals of bodily exercise: but still the high-pressure system goes on; and, with all their attainments in the way of learning, few of the young ladies who return home after a highly-finished education, are possessed of health and energy sufficient to make use of their attainments, even if they occupied a field more suited to their display.

I know not how it may affect others, but the number of languid, listless, and inert young ladies, who now recline upon our sofas, murmuring and repining at every claim upon their personal exertions, is to me a truly melancholy spectacle, and one which demands the attention of a benevolent and enlightened public, even more, perhaps, than some of those great national schemes in which the people and the government are alike interested. It is but rarely now that we meet with a really healthy woman; and, highly as intellectual attainments may be prized, I think all will allow that no qualifications can be of much value without the power of bringing them into use.

The difference I would point out, between the exercise of the intellect and that of the moral feelings is this. It has so pleased the all-wise Disposer of our lives, that the duties he has laid down for the right government of the human family, have in their very nature something that expands and invigorates the soul; so that instead of being weary of well-doing, the character becomes strengthened, the energies enlivened, and the whole sphere of capability enlarged.

Who has not felt, after a long, conflict between duty and inclination, when at last the determination has been formed, and duty has been submitted to, not grudgingly, but from very love to the Father of mercies, who alone can judge what will eventually promote the good of his weak, erring, and short-sighted creatures—from reverence for his holy laws, and from gratitude to the Saviour of mankind; —who has not felt a sudden impulse of thanksgiving and delight as they were enabled to make this decision, a springing up, as it were, of the soul from the low cares and entanglements of this world, to a higher and purer state of existence, where the motives and feelings under which the choice has been made, will be appreciated and approved, but where every inducement that could have been brought forward to vindicate a different choice, would have been rejected at the bar of eternal justice?

It is not the applause of man that can reach the heart under such circumstances. No human eye is wished for, to look in upon our self-denial, or to witness the sacrifice we make. The good we have attempted to do may even fail in its effect. We know that the result is not with us, but with Him who seeth in secret, and who has left us in possession of this encouraging assurance, Inasmuch as ye do it unto one of these, ye do it onto me.

Was the human mind ever enfeebled, or the human frame exhausted, by feelings of kindness? No! The hour of true refreshment and invigoration is that in which we do our duty, whatever it may be, cheerfully and humbly, as in the sight of God; not pluming ourselves upon our own merit, or anticipating great results, but with a childlike dependence upon his promises, and devout aspirations to be ever employed in working out his holy will.

In the pursuit of intellectual attainments, we cannot encourage ourselves throughout the day, nor revive our wearied energies at night, by saying, "It is for the love of my heavenly Father that I do this. " But, as a very little child may be taught, for the love of a lost parent, to avoid what that parent would have disapproved; so the young may be cheered and led onward in the path of duty by the same principle, connecting every action of their lives in which good and evil may be blended, with the condemnation or approval of their Father who is in heaven.

There is no principle in our nature which at the same time softens and ennobles, subdues and exalts, so much as the principle of gratitude; and it ought ever to be remembered, in numbering our blessings, that gratitude has been made the foundation of Christian morality. The ancient philosophers had their system of morals, and a beautiful one it was. But it had this defect—it had no sure foundation; sometimes shifting from expediency to the rights of man, and thus having no fixed and determinate character. The happier system under which we are privileged to live, has all the advantages acknowledged by the philosophers of old, with this great and merciful addition, that it is peculiarly calculated to wind itself in with our affections, by being founded upon gratitude, and thus to excite, in connexion with the practice of all it enjoins, those emotions of mind which are most conducive to our happiness.

Let us imagine a little community of young women, amongst whom, to do an act of disinterested kindness should be an object of the highest ambition, and where to do any act of pure selfishness, tending, however remotely, to the injury of another, should be regarded as the deepest disgrace; where they should be accustomed to consider their time not as their own, but lent them solely for the purpose of benefiting their fellow-creatures; and where those who were known to exercise the greatest charity and forbearance, should be looked upon as the most exalted individual in the whole community. Would these girls be weary? Would they be discontented, listless, and inanimate? The experiment remains to be tried.

It is a frequent and popular remark, that girls are less trouble to manage in families than boys; and so unquestionably they are. But when their parents go on to say that girls awaken less anxiety, are safer and more easily brought up, I am disposed to think such parents look with too superficial a view to the conduct of their children before the world, rather than the state of their hearts before God.

It is true that girls have little temptation, generally speaking, to vice. They are so hemmed in and guarded by the rules of society, that they must be destitute almost of the common feelings of human nature, to be willing, for any consideration, to sacrifice their good name. But do such parents ever ask, how much of evil may be cherished and indulged in, and the good name retained? I am aware that amongst the generality of women there is more religious feeling than amongst men, more observance of the ordinances of religion, more reading of the scriptures, and more attention to the means of religious information. But let not the woman who sits in peace, and unassailed by temptation, in the quiet retirement of her own parlour, look down with self-complacency and contempt upon the open transgressions of her erring brother. Rather let her weigh in the scale his strong passions, and strong inducements to evil, and, it may be, strong compunctions too, against her own little envyings, bickerings, secret spite, and soul-cherished idolatry of self; and then ask of her conscience which is farthest in advance towards the kingdom of heaven.

It is true, she has uttered no profane expression, but she has set afloat upon a winged whisper the transgression of her neighbour. She has polluted her lips with no intoxicating draught, but she has drunk of the Circean cup of flattery, and acted from vanity and self-love, when she was professing to act from higher motives. She has run into no excesses but the excess of display; and she has injured no one by her bad example, except in the practice of petty faults. In short, she has not sinned beyond her own temptations.

One of the most striking features in the character of the young ladies of the present day, is the absence of contentment. They are lively when excited, but no sooner does the excitement cease, than they fall back into their habitual listlessness, under which they so often complain of their fate, and speak of themselves as unfortunate and afflicted, that one would suppose them to be victims of adversity, did not a more intimate acquaintance with their actual circumstances, convince us that they were surrounded by every thing conducive to rational comfort. For the sake of the poetry of the matter, one would scarcely deny to every young lady her little canker-worm to nurse in her bosom, since all must have their pets. But when they add selfishness to melancholy, and trouble their friends with their idle and fruitless complaints, the case becomes too serious for a jest. Indeed, I am not sure that the professing Christian, who rises every morning with a cherished distaste for the duties of the day, who turns away when they present themselves, under a belief that they are more difficult or more disgusting than the duties of other people, who regards her own allotment in the world as peculiarly hard, and never pours forth her soul in devout thanksgiving for the blessings she enjoys, is not in reality as culpable in the sight of God, and living as much at variance with the spirit of true religion, as the individual who spends the same portion of time in the practice of more open and palpable sin.

It is an undeniable improvement in modern education, that religious instruction is becoming more general, that pupils are questioned in the knowledge of the Scriptures, instructed in the truths of religion, and sent forth into the world prepared to give an answer respecting the general outlines of Christianity. So long, however, as the discontent above alluded to remains so prevalent, we must question the sufficiency of this method of instruction; and it is under a strong conviction, that to teach young people to talk about religion is but a small part of what is necessary to the establishment of their christian characters, that I have ventured to put forth what may be regarded as crude remarks upon this important subject.

I still cling fondly to the hope, that, ere long, some system of female instruction will be discovered, by which the young women of England may be sent home from school prepared for the stations appointed them by Providence to fill in after life, and prepared to fill them well. Then indeed may this favoured country boast of her privileges, when her young women return to their homes and their parents, habituated to be on the watch for every opportunity of doing good to others; making it the first and the last inquiry of every day, "What can I do to make my parents, my brothers, or my sisters, more happy? I am but a feeble instrument in the hands of Providence, to work out any of his benevolent designs; but as he will give me strength, I hope to pursue the plan to which I have been accustomed, of seeking my own happiness only in the happiness of others. "

CHAPTER IV. DRESS AND MANNERS.

THAT the extent of woman's influence is not always commensurate with the cultivation of her intellectual powers, is a truth which the experience and observation of every day tend to confirm; for how often do we find that a lavish expenditure upon the means of acquiring knowledge, is productive of no adequate result in the way of lessening the sum of human misery.

When we examine the real state of society, and single out the individuals whose habits, conversation, and character produce the happiest effect upon their fellow-creatures, we invariably find them persons who are morally, rather than intellectually great; and consequently the possession of genius is, to a woman, a birthright of very ques- tionable value. It is a remark, not always charitably made, but unfortunately too true, that the most talented women are not the most agreeable in their domestic capacity; and frequent and unsparing are the batteries of sarcasm and wit, which consequently open upon our unfortunate blues? It should be remembered, however, that the evil is not in the presence of one quality, but in the absence of another; and we ought never to forget the redeeming excellence of those signal instances, in which the moral worth of the female character is increased and supported by intellectual power. If, in order to maintain a beneficial influence in society, superior talent, or even a high degree of learning, were required, solitary and insignificant would be the lot of some of the most social, benevolent, and noble-hearted women, who now occupy the very centre of attraction within their respective circles, and claim from all around them a just and appropriate tribute of affection and esteem.

It need scarcely be repeated, that although great intellectual attainments are by no means the highest recommendation that a woman can possess, the opposite extreme of ignorance, or natural imbecility of mind, are effectual barriers to the exercise of any considerable degree of influence in society. An ignorant woman who has not the good sense to keep silent, or a weak woman pleased with her own prattle, are scarcely less annoying than humiliating to those who, from acquaintance or family connexion, have the misfortune to be identified with them; yet it is surprising how far a small measure of talent, or of mental cultivation, may be made to extend in the way of giving pleasure, when accompanied by good taste, good sense, and good feeling, especially with that feeling which leads the mind from self and selfish motives, into an habitual regard to the good and the happiness of others.

The more we reflect upon this subject, the more we must be convinced, that there is a system of discipline required for women, totally distinct from what is called the learning of the schools, and that, unless they can be prepared for their allotment in life by some process calculated to fit them for performing its domestic duties, the time bestowed upon their education will be found, in after life, to have been wholly inadequate to procure for them either habits of usefulness, or a healthy tone of mind.

It would appear from a superficial observation of the views of domestic and social duty about to be presented, that in the estimation of the writer, the great business of a woman's life was to make herself agreeable; for so minute are some of the points which properly engage her attention, that they scarcely seem to bear upon the great object of doing good. Yet when we reflect that by giving pleasure in an innocent and unostentatious manner, innumerable channels are opened for administering instruction, assistance, or consolation, we cease to regard as insignificant the smallest of those means by which a woman can render herself an object either of affection or disgust.

First, then, and most familiar to common observation, is her personal appearance; and in this case, vanity, more potent in woman's heart than selfishness, renders it an object of general solicitude to be so adorned as best to meet and gratify the public taste. Without inquiring too minutely into the motive, the custom, as such, must be commended; for, like many of the minor virtues of women, though scarcely taken note of in its immediate presence, it is sorely missed when absent. A careless or slatternly woman, for instance, is one of the most repulsive objects in creation; and such is the force of public opinion in favour of the delicacies of taste and feeling in the female sex, that no power of intellect, or dis- play of learning, can compensate to men, for the want of nicety or neatness in the women with whom they associate in domestic life. In vain to them might the wreath of laurel wave in glorious triumph over locks uncombed; and wo betide the heroine, whose stocking, even of the deepest blue, betrayed a lurking hole!

It is, however, a subject too serious for jest, and ought to be regarded by all women with earnest solicitude that they may constantly maintain in their own persons that strict attention to good taste and delicacy of feeling, which affords the surest evidence of delicacy of mind; a quality without which no woman ever was, or ever will be, charming. Let her appear in company with what accomplishments she may, let her charm by her musical talents, attract by her beauty, or enliven by her wit, if there steal from underneath her graceful drapery, the soiled hem, the tattered frill, or even the coarse garment out of keeping with her external finery, imagination naturally carries the observer to her dressing-room, her private habits, and even to her inner mind, where, it is almost impossible to believe that the same want of order and purity does not prevail.

It is a prevalent but most injurious mistake, to suppose that all women must be splendidly and expensively dressed, to recommend themselves to general approbation. In order to do this, how many, in the sphere of life to which these remarks apply, are literally destitute of comfort both in their hearts, and in their homes; for the struggle between parents and children, to raise the means on one hand, and to obtain them either by argument or subterfuge on the other, is but one amongst the many sources of family discord and individual suffering, which mark out the excess of artificial wants as the great evil of the present times.

A very slight acquaintance with the sentiments and tone of conversation familiar amongst men, might convince all whose minds are open to conviction, that their admiration is not to be obtained by the display of any kind of extravagance in dress. There may be occasional instances of the contrary, but the praise most liberally and uniformly bestowed by men upon the dress of women, is, that it is neat, becoming, or in good taste.

The human mind is often influenced by association, while immediate impression is all that it takes cognizance of at the moment. Thus a splendidly dressed woman entering the parlour of a farm-house, or a tradesman's drawing-room, bursts upon the sight as an astounding and almost monstrous spectacle; and we are scarcely aware that the repulsion we instantaneously experience, arises from a secret conviction of how much the gorgeous fabric must have cost the wearer, in time, and thought, and money; especially when we know that the same individual is under the necessity of spending her morning hours in culinary operations, and is, or ought to be, the sharer of her husband's daily toil.

There is scarcely any object in art or nature, calculated to excite our admiration, which may not, from being ill-placed, excite our ridicule or disgust. Each individual article of clothing worn by this woman, may be superb in itself, but there is a want of fitness and harmony in the whole, from which we turn away.

Perhaps there are no single objects in themselves so beautiful as flowers, and it might seem difficult to find a situation in which they could be otherwise; yet I have seen—and seen with a feeling almost like pity—at the conclusion of a feast, fair rose-leaves and sweet jessamine floating amidst such inappropriate elements, that all their beauty was despoiled, and they were fit only to be cast away with the refuse of gross matter in which they were involved.

Admiration of a beautiful object, how intense soever it may be, cannot impart that high tone of intellectual enjoyment which arises from our admiration of fitness and beauty combined; and thus the richest silk, and the finest lace, when inappropriately worn, are beautifully manufactured articles, but nothing more. While, therefore, on the one hand, there is a moral degradation in the consciousness of wearing soiled or disreputable garments, or in being in any way below the average of personal decency; there is, on the other, a gross violation of good taste, in assuming for the middle classes of society, whose occupations are closely connected with the means of bodily subsistence, the same description of personal ornament, as belongs with more propriety to those who enjoy the luxury of giving orders, without any necessity for farther occupation of time or thought.

The most frequently recurring perplexities of woman's life arise from cases which religion does not immediately reach, and in which she is still expected to decide properly, and act agreeably without any other law than that of good taste for her guide. Good taste is therefore most essential to the regulation of her dress and general appearance; and wherever any striking violation of this principle appears, the beholder is immediately impressed with the idea that a very important rule of her life and conduct is wanting. It is not all who possess this guide within themselves; but an attentive observation of human life and character, especially a due regard to the beauty of fitness, would enable all to avoid giving offence in this particular way.

The regard to fitness here recommended, is a duty of much more serious importance than would at first sight appear, since it involves a consideration which cannot too often be presented to the mind, of what, and who we are? —what is the station we are appointed to fill, and what the objects for which we are living!

Behold yon gorgeous fabric in the distance, with its rainbow hues, and gems, and shining drapery, "And flowers the fairest that might feast the bee. " A coronet of beauty crowns the whole, and feathery ornaments, on frail silvery threads, glitter, and wave, and tremble at every moving breath. Surely the countenance of Flora blooms below, and Zephyrus suspends his gentle wings at her approach. The spectacle advances. It is not health, nor youth, nor beauty, that we see; but poor, decrepit, helpless, miserable old age. We gaze, and a shudder comes over us, for Death is grinning in the back-ground, and we hear his voice triumphantly exclaiming, "This is mine! "

Look at that moving garden, and those waving plumes, as they pass along the aisle of the church or the chapel. They form the adornment of a professedly christian woman, the mother of a family; and this is the day appointed for partaking of that ordinance to which Christians are invited to come in meekness and lowliness of spirit, to commemorate the love of their Redeemer, who, though he was rich, for their sakes became poor—who humbled himself, and became obedient unto death, to purchase their exemption from the penalty of sin, and the bondage of the world.

We would earnestly hope that, in the greater number of such cases as these, the error is in the judgment—the mockery thoughtlessly assumed: but would not the habit of self-examination, followed up by serious inquiry respecting our real and individual position in society, as moral agents and immortal beings, be a likely means of averting the ridicule that age is ill prepared to bear; and, what is of infinitely more consequence, of preventing the scandal that religion has too much cause to charge upon her friends?

It frequently happens that women in the middle class of society are not entirely free from provincialisms in their manner of speaking, as well as other peculiarities, by which it may easily be discovered that their interests are local, and their means of information of limited extent; in short, that they are persons who have but little acquaintance with the polite or fashionable world; and yet they may be persons highly estimable and important in their own sphere. Very little either of esteem or importance, however, attaches to their characters, where their ingenuity is taxed to maintain what they believe to be a fashionable or elegant exterior, and which, in connexion with their unpolished dialect and homely occupations, renders them but too much like the chimney-sweepers' queen decked out for a May-day exhibition. The invidious question unavoidably occurs to the beholder—for what or for whom has such a person mistaken herself? while, had she been dressed in a plain substantial costume, corresponding with her mind and habits, she might have been known at once, and respected for what she really was, —a rational, independent, and valuable member of society.

It is not, by any means, the smallest of the services required by christian charity, to point out to our fellow-countrywomen how they may avoid being ridiculous. Perhaps a higher degree of intellectual dignity would raise us all above the weakness of being moved to laughter by so slight a cause. But such is the constitution of the general order of minds, that they are less entertained by the most pointed witticisms, than by those striking contrasts and discrepancies, which seem to imply that rusticity has mistaken itself for elegance, deformity for beauty, age for youth. I pretend not to defend this propensity to turn so serious a mistake into jest. I merely say that such a propensity does exist, and, what is amongst the anomalies of our nature, that it sometimes exhibits itself most unreservedly in the very individuals who in their turn are furnishing food for merriment to others.

The laughing philosopher might have reasoned thus, "Let them all laugh on, they will cure each other. " But the question is—does ridicule correct the evil? Most assuredly it does not. It does something more, however. It rankles like a poison in the bosom where it falls, and destroys the peace of many an amiable but ill-judging candidate for public admiration. Women, especially, are its victims and its prey; and well do they learn, under the secret tutelage of envy, jealousy, and pride, how to make this engine of discord play upon each other.

When we listen to the familiar conversation of women, especially of those whose minds are tainted by vulgarity, and unenlightened by the higher principles of religion, we find that a very large portion of their time and attention is bestowed upon the subject of dress—not of their own dress merely, but of that of their neighbours; and in drawing conclusions, the most critical and minute, from the precise grade of gentility which such individuals are supposed to assume. Looking farther, we find, what is more astonishing, that there exists in connexion with the same subject a degree of rivalry and ambition which call forth many of the evil passions that are ever ready to spring into action, and mar the pleasant pictures of social life. In awakening these, the ridicule already alluded to is a powerful agent; for, like the most injurious of libels, it adheres so nearly to the truth, as to set contradiction at defiance. Thus, there are few persons who would not rather be maligned than ridiculed; and thus the wounds indicted by ridicule are the most difficult to heal, and the last to be forgiven.

Surely, then, it is worth paying some regard to the principles of fitness and consistency, in order to avoid the consequences necessarily resulting from every striking deviation from these rules; and the women of England possess many advantages in the cultivation of their natural powers of discrimination and reason, for enabling them to ascertain the precise position of this line of conduct, which it is so important to them to observe. They are free from many of the national prejudices entertained by the women of other countries, and they enjoy the inestimable privilege of being taught to look up to a higher standard of morals, for the right guidance of their conduct. It is to them, therefore, that we look for what rational and useful women ought to be, not only in the essentials of christian character, but in the minor points of social, domestic, and individual duty.

Much that has been said on the subject of dress, is equally applicable to that of manners. Fitness, and adaptation, are here, as well as in the former instance, the general rule; for of what value is elegance in a cottage, or the display of animal strength at a European court?

In the middle walks of life, an easy manner, free from affectation on the one hand, and grossness on the other, is all that is required; and such are, or ought to be, the occupations of all women of this class, as most happily to induce such habits of activity and free-agency, as would effectually preserve them from the two extremes of coldness and frivolous absurdity.

The grand error of the day seems to be, that of calling themselves ladies, when it ought to be their ambition to be women, —women who fill a place, and occupy a post—members of the commonwealth—supporters of the fabric of society, —the minor wheels and secret springs of the great machine of human life and action, which cannot move harmoniously, nor with full effect to the accomplishment of any great or noble purpose, while clogged with the lovely burdens, and impeded by the still-life attitudes of those useless members of the community, who cast themselves about on every hand, in the vain hope of being valued and admired for doing nothing.

Amongst the changes introduced by modern taste, it is not the least striking, that all the daughters of trades-people, when sent to school, are no longer girls, but young ladies. The linen-draper whose worthy consort occupies her daily post behind the counter, receives her child from Mrs. Montague's establishment—a young lady. At the same elegant and expensive seminary, music and Italian are taught to Hannah Smith, whose father deals in Yarmouth herrings; and there is the butcher's daughter, too, perhaps the most ladylike of them all. The manners of these young ladies naturally take their tone and character from the ridiculous assumptions of modern refinement. The butcher's daughter is seized with nausea at the spectacle of raw meat—Hannah Smith is incapable of existing, within the atmosphere of her father's home—and the child of the linen-draper elopes with a merchant's clerk, to avoid the dire necessity of assisting in her father's shop.

What a catalogue of miseries might be made out, as the consequence of this mistaken ambition of the women of England to be ladies! Gentlewomen they may be, and refined women too; for when did either gentleness or true refinement disqualify a woman for her proper duties? But that assumption of delicacy which unfits them for the real business of life, is more to be dreaded in its fatal influence upon their happiness, than the most agonizing disease with which they could be afflicted.

It is needless to say that women of this morbid, imbecile character have no influence. They are so occupied with the minutiæ of their own personal miseries, that they have no time to think of the sin and the sorrow existing in the world around them. Whatever is proposed to them in the way of doing good, is sure to meet with a listless, weary, murmuring denial: for if the hundred-and-one objections, arising out of other fancied causes, should be obviated, there are their endless and inexhaustible nerves. Alas! alas! that English women should ever have found themselves out to be possessed of nerves! Not the most exquisite creation of the poet's fancy was ever supposed to be more susceptible of pain, than is now the highly-educated young lady, who reclines upon a couch in an apartment slightly separated from that in which her father sells his goods, and but one remove from the sphere of her mother's culinary toil.

How different from this feeble, discontented, helpless thing, is the woman who shows by her noble bearing that she knows her true position in society; and who knows, also, that the virtue and the value attaching to her character must be in exact proportion to the benefit she confers upon her fellow-creatures; —above all, who feels that the only Being who is capable of knowing what is ultimately best, has seen meet to place her exactly where the powers of her mind and the purposes of her life may be made most conducive to his merciful and wise designs. Not the meanest habiliments, nor the most homely personal aspect, can conceal the worth and dignity of such a woman; and whatever that position with which she has made herself so well acquainted may be, she will find that her influence extends to its remotest circle.

It is impossible to say what the manners of such a woman are. In the cottage, in the court, in the daily and hourly performance of social services, they are, and must be, characterised by the same attributes—general adaptation supported by dignity, a high sense of duty predominating over every tendency to selfish indulgence, and prompting to the performance of every kind of practical good, a degree of self-respect, without which no talent can be matured, and no purpose rendered firm; yet, along with this, a far higher degree of respect for others, exhibited in modes of deference, and acts of consideration as various as the different characters whose good or whose happiness are the subjects of her care; and, lastly, that sweet sister of benevolence, charity, without which no woman ever yet could make herself a desirable companion or friend.

It may be said that these are virtues, not modes of conduct; but how much of virtue, particularly that of charity, may be implied and understood by what is commonly called manner. That which in the present day is considered the highest attainment in this branch of conduct, is, a lady-like manner, and it is one that well deserves the attention of all who wish to recommend themselves—who wish, as all must do, to ward off insulting familiarity, and court respectful consideration. There are, however, many impressions conveyed to the minds of others by mere manner, far exceeding this in interest and importance. What, for instance, is so consoling to the afflicted as a sympathizing manner? The direct expression of sympathy might possibly give pain; but there is a manner, and happy are they who possess it, which conveys a silent invitation to the sorrowing soul to unburden its griefs, with an assurance that it may do so without fear of treachery or unkindness. There seems to be an instinct in our nature by which this mode of expressing sympathy is rendered intelligible; and who that has any thing to do with sorrow or suffering, or any wish to alleviate the pressure of either, would not desire that their manner should be so fraught with sympathy, as to impart the consolation they may be unable to express in words?

Who, on the other hand, in a world which all the afflicted are disposed to consider cold and unfeeling, has not felt what it was, to meet with that peculiar tone of voice, that long, earnest gaze of the eye, and that watchfulness of personal comfort, which belong to a degree of interest deeper than can be told, and which convince, beyond the power of language, that we are not—we cannot be overlooked or forgotten? How many an alien has been invited to return by a look, a tone, a gesture, when no power of speech would have conveyed the same impression of a welcome! How many a prejudice has been overcome—how many a dangerous resolution broken—how many a dark design defeated by a conciliating and confiding manner! and may it not also be asked, how many an insult has been repelled by a manner fraught with dignity; how many an injury has been returned into the bosom where it originated, by a manner which conveyed all the bitterness of cherished and determined revenge?

To those who make the human mind their study, the mode of acting is of more importance than the action itself; and to women it is especially so, because the sphere in which they actually move is comparatively limited and obscure. It is seldom regarded as consistent with that delicacy which forms so great a charm in their nature, that they should act out to their full extent all the deep feelings of which they are capable. Thus there is no other channel for their perpetual overflow, than that of their manners; and thus a sensitive and ingenious woman can exhibit much of her own character, and lead others out into the display of much of theirs, simply by the instrumentality of her manners; and, upon the same principle, that good breeding which obtains the highest applause in society, is but an imitation or assumption of every moral excellence, depicted on a minor scale.

Good manners are the small-coin of virtue, distributed abroad as an earnest—we will not ask how fallacious—of the greater and better things that lie beyond. The women of England are becoming increasingly solicitous about their manners, that they may in all points resemble such as prevail in a higher circle of society, and be, consequently, the best. But would it not be more advantageous to them, to bestow the same increase of solicitude upon what constitutes the true foundation of all that is amiable and excellent in life and conduct? Would it not be more advantageous to them to remember, that in the sphere of life appointed for them to fill, stronger and more efficient traits of character are required, than can possibly be classed under the epithet of ladylike? Not that coarseness or vulgarity of manner could ever be tolerated in those delicate intimacies, and intellectual associations, which properly belong to the class of women of whom England had once a right to boast— intimacies and associations, intervening, like gleams of sunshine, between their seasons of perplexity and care; but the manners I would earnestly recommend to my countrywomen are of a character calculated to convey an idea of much more than refinement; they are manners to which a high degree of moral influence belongs, inasmuch as they inspire confidence, command esteem, and contribute to the general sum of human happiness.

Adaptation is the leading feature in this class of manners— adaptation, not only to the circumstances of the person who acts and speaks, but also to the circumstances of those upon whom such speech or action operates. A light, careless, sportive manner is sometimes thought exceedingly charming; and when it emanates from youth and innocence, can scarcely fail to please; but when such a manner is affected by a woman of ponderous personal weight, of naturally grave countenance, and responsible station in society, none can avoid being struck with the obvious anomaly, and few can avoid being moved to laughter or contempt.

In English society it frequently happens that persons of humble parentage, and homely station, in early life, are raised, by the acquisition of wealth, to the enjoyment of luxurious indulgence. How absurd in such cases, is that assumption of delicacy and of aristocratic dignity, which we too often see, and which is sure to give rise to every variety of uncharitable remark upon what they and their families have been.

Self-importance, or rather a prevailing consciousness of self, is the most universal hinderance to the attainment of agreeable manners. A woman of delicate feelings and cultivated mind, who goes into company determined to be interested, rather than to interest, can scarcely fail to please. We are assured, however, that in this respect there is something very defective in the present state of society. All desire to make an impression, none to be impressed; and thus the social intercourse of every day is rendered wearisome if not disgusting, by the constant struggle of each contending party to assume the same relative position.

An instance relating immediately to an animal of inferior grade in the creation to man, but bearing some affinity to the case in point, is told by a traveller, whose party having shot several old monkeys, took home their young ones to the camp where he was stationed. He amused himself in the evening by watching these little animals, which had been so accustomed to be caressed and carried about by their parents, that they expected the same services from each other, and by their persevering efforts to obtain assistance from those who in an equal degree required it from them, formed themselves into a tumultuous heap, and nearly worried each other to death.

It might be invidious to compare the tumult of feeling, the weariness, and the fatality to happiness experienced by these animals, to that which is produced by the general desire to make an impression, in modern society; but none can be blind to the fact, that a determination to be pleased in company, is the surest means of giving pleasure, as well as of receiving it.

A young lady who has not had an opportunity of conversing, of playing, or of showing off in any other way, is almost sure to return from an evening party complaining of its dulness, and discontented with herself, as well as with everyone beside. Ask her if such and such agreeable and intelligent persons were not present; and she answers, "Yes. " Ask her if they did not converse, and converse pleasantly; and still she answers, "Yes. " What then? The fact is, she has herself made no impression, charmed nobody, and therefore, as a necessary consequence, she is not charmed.

How much more happiness does that woman experience, who, when in company, directs her attention to her nearest neighbour; and, beholding a cheerful countenance, or hearing a pleasant voice, is encouraged to proceed in cultivating an acquaintance, which may ultimately ripen into friendship, may teach her some useful lesson, or raise her estimate of her fellow-creatures. Even where no such agreeable results are experienced, where the party attempted proves wholly impracticable, there is still a satisfaction in having made the trial, far beyond what can be experienced by any defeated attempt to be agreeable. Indeed, the disappointment of having failed to make a pleasing impression, merely for the purpose of gratifying our own vanity, without reference to the happiness of others, is adapted in an especial manner to sour the temper, and depress the mind; because we feel, along with the disappointment, a mortifying consciousness that our ambition has been of an undignified and selfish kind; while, if our endeavour has been to contribute to the general sum of social enjoyment, by encouraging the diffident, cultivating the acquaintance of the amiable, and stimulating latent talent, we cannot feel depressed by such a failure, nor mortified at our want of success.

The great question with regard to modern education is, which of these two classes of feeling does it instil into the mind—does it inspire the young women of the present day with an amiable desire to make every body happy around them? or does it teach them only to sing, and play, and speak in foreign languages, and consequently leave them to be the prey of their own disappointed feelings, whenever they find it impossible to make any of these qualifications tell upon society?

CHAPTER V. CONVERSATION OF THE WOMEN OF ENGLAND.

IT may not, perhaps, be asking too much of the reader, to request that gentle personage to bear in mind, that in speaking both of the characteristics and the influence of a certain class of females, strict reference has been maintained, throughout the four preceding CHAPTERs, to such as may with justice be denominated true English women. With puerile exotics, bending from their own feebleness, and wandering like weeds, about the British garden, to the hinderance of the growth of all useful plants, this work has little to do, except to point out how they might have been cultivated to better purpose.

I have said of English women, that they are the best fire-side companions; but I am afraid that my remark must apply to a very small portion of the community at large. The number of those who are wholly destitute of the highest charm belonging to social companionship, is lamentably great: and these pages would never have been obtruded upon the notice of the public, had there not been strong symptoms of the number becoming greater still.

Women have the choice of many means of bringing their principles into exercise, and of obtaining influence, both in their own domestic sphere, and in society at large. Amongst the most important of these is conversation; an engine so powerful upon the minds and characters of mankind in general, that beauty fades before it, and wealth in comparison is but as leaden coin. If match-making were indeed the great object of human life, I should scarcely dare to make this assertion, since few men choose women for their conversation, where wealth or beauty are to be had. I must, however, think more nobly of the female sex, and believe them more solicitous to maintain affection after the match is made, than simply to be led to the altar, as wives whose influence will that day be laid aside with their wreaths of white roses, and laid aside for ever.

If beauty or wealth have been the bait in this connexion, the bride may gather up her wreath of roses, and place them again upon her polished brow; nay, she may bestow the treasures of her wealth without reserve, and permit the husband of her choice to "spoil her goodly lands, to gild his waste; " she may do what she will—dress, bloom, or descend from affluence to poverty; but if she has no intellectual hold upon her husband's heart, she must inevitably become that most helpless and pitiable of earthly objects—a slighted wife.

Conversation, understood in its proper character, as distinct from mere talk, might rescue her from this. Not conversation upon books, if her husband happens to be a fox-hunter; nor upon fox-hunting, if he is a book-worm; but exactly that kind of conversation which is best adapted to his tastes and habits, yet at the same time capable of leading him a little out of both into a wider field of observation, and subjects he may never have derived amusement from before, simply from the fact of their never having been presented to his notice.

How pleasantly the evening hours may be made to pass, when a woman who really can converse, will thus beguile the time. But, on the other hand, how wretched is the portion of that man who dreads the dulness of his own fireside! who sees the clog of his existence ever seated there—the same, in the deadening influence she has upon his spirits to-day, as yesterday, to-morrow, and the next day, and the next! Welcome, thrice welcome, is the often-invited visiter, who breaks the dismal dual of this scene.

Married women are often spoken of in high terms of commendation for their personal services, their handiwork, and their domestic management; but I am inclined to think that a married woman, possessing all these, and even beauty too, yet wanting conversation, might become "weary, stale, flat, and unprofitable, " in the estimation of her husband; and, finally, might drive him from his home by the leaden weight of her uncompanionable society.

I know not whether other minds have felt the same as mine under the pressure of some personal presence without fellowship of feeling. Innocent and harmless the individual may be who thus inflicts the grievance, yet there is an irksomeness in their mere bodily presence, almost intolerable to be borne; and in proportion to the estimate we form of real society, and companionship, and sympathy of feeling, is the dread we entertain of association with mere animal life in its human form, while nothing of this fellowship of feeling is experienced.

There cannot, however, be a greater mistake in the science of being agreeable, than to suppose that conversation must be made a business of. Oh! the misery of being pitted against a professional converser! —one who looks from side to side until a vacant ear is found, and commences a battery of declamation if you will not answer, and of argument if you will. Indeed the immense variety of annoyances deducible from ill-managed conversation, are a sufficient proof of its importance in society; and any one disposed to dispute this fact, need only recall the many familiar instances of disappointment and chagrin, which all who mix in any manner with what is called the world, must have experienced, from mistaken views of what is agreeable in conversation.

It would be vain to attempt an enumeration of the different aspects under which this peculiar kind of annoyance presents itself. A few heads will be sufficient for the different classes of injudicious talkers. First, then, we naturally think of those who have obtained the conventional appellation of bores; or, to describe them more politely, the class of talkers whose over-solicitude is proportioned to their difficulty in obtaining patient hearers. These, again, may be subdivided into endless varieties, of which a few specimens will suffice. Yet amongst all these, even the most inveterate, may be found worthy individuals, whose qualifications for imparting both instruction and amusement are by no means contemptible.

Entitled to distinction in the art of annoyance are the hobby-riders— those who not only ride a favourite hobby themselves, but expect every one they meet with to mount and ride the same. It matters not whether their ruling subject be painting or politics, except that minds devoted to the fine arts have generally about them some delicacy as to the reception of their favourites, and are too shrinkingly alive to the slights they may receive, to risk their introduction without some indication of a welcome. Still there are exceptions even to this rule, and nothing can be more wearisome to the uninitiated, or more unintelligible to the unpractised ear, than the jargon poured forth by an amateur painter without regard to the tastes or the understandings of those around him.

Perhaps his fellow-traveller is seated on some gentle eminence, drinking in the deep quiet of a summer's evening, not merely from sight, but sound, and blending all with treasured memories of the past, in which no stranger could intermeddle, when the painter bursts upon him with his technicalities, and the illusion is gone. He raves about the breadth of the colouring. His companion sees the long tall shadows of the trees reflected on the sloping green, with the golden sunset gleaming in between the stems, and through the interstices of the foliage, and he knows not where the poetry or even the truth of this wonderful property of breadth can be. The painter descants upon the bringing out of the distant cottage from the wood. His companion is of opinion it would be better to let it remain where it is—half hid in the retirement of the forest, and sending up, as it seems, from the very bosom of the silent shade, its wreath of curling smoke to indicate the social scene beneath its rustic roof, prepared for, by the lighting of the woodman's fire. But the painter is not satisfied. He calls upon his friend to observe the grouping of the whole. He must have the outline broken. The thing is done. His sketch is exhibited in triumph, and he raves on, with accelerated delight, for he has cleft the hills in twain, and placed a group of robbers on the broken ground. Alas! how should his companion believe or understand! His thoughts are expatiating upon that scene, because its sloping hills, and cultivated fields, and gardens, and orchards, and village churchyard, are like the spot where he was born, and where his father died—and he sees no mountain gorge, nor bandit chief, nor hears the rush of torrents on the breeze; but his eye dwells again upon the apple-tree in its spring-bloom, and the lambs upon the lea, and his ear is open to the cooing of the wood-pigeon on the chestnut boughs, and the sound of voices—than all other sounds more sweet—the voices that spoke kindly to his childhood.

It might be supposed that, if under any circumstances the society of a painter could be always welcome, it would be amongst the varied scenes of a picturesque tour. But even here the mind has pictures of its own, and he who is perpetually telling you what to see, might as well force upon you at every view, the use of his camera lucida, and neither allow you to gaze upon nature as you wish to behold it, nor as it really is.

Women are perhaps less addicted than men to annoy others with their pet subjects; because they have less opportunity of following out any particular branch of art or study, to the exclusion of others; and politics, that most prevalent and unceasing absorbent of conversation, is seldom a favourite theme with them. They have, however, their houses and their servants, and, what is infinitely worse—they have themselves.

Perhaps accustomed to a little private admiration in a remote corner of the world, they obtain a false estimate of their own importance, and act as if they thought no subject so interesting as that which turns upon their own experience, their own peculiarities, or even their own faults. It does not always follow that such women admire themselves so much as the prevalence of self in their conversation would at first lead us to suppose, for in expatiating upon the good qualities of others, they often exclaim—and why should we doubt their sincerity? —how much they wish they were like the beings they extol! They will even speak disparagingly of themselves, and tell of their own faults without occasion; but even while they do this with an air of humility, they seldom fail to leave an impression on the minds of their hearers, that in reality they like their own faults better than the virtues of others.

It is not of much consequence what is the nature of the subject proposed to the attention of this class of talkers. If the weather: "It does not agree with me, I like the wind from the west. " If the politics of the country in which they live: "I have not given much attention to politics, nor do I think that women should. " If any moral quality in the abstract is discussed: "Oh, that is just my fault! " or, "If I possess any virtue, I do think it is that. " If an anecdote is related: "That is like [or not like] me. I should [or should not] have done the same. " If the beauty of any distant place is described: "I never was there, but my uncle once was within ten miles of it; and had it not been for the miscarriage of a letter, I should have been his companion in that journey. My uncle was always fond of taking me with him. Dear good man, I was a great pet of his. " If the lapse of time is the subject of conversation: "The character undergoes many changes in a few years. I wonder whether, or in what way, mine will be altered two years hence. " If the moon: "How many people write sonnets to the moon. I never did. "

And thus sun, moon, and stars—the whole created universe—are but links in that continuous chain which vibrates with perpetual music to the egotist, connecting all things in heaven and earth, however discordant or heterogeneous, by a perfect and harmonious union with self.

A very slight degree of observation would enable such individuals to perceive that as soon as self is put in the place of any of the subjects in question, conversation necessarily flags, as this topic, to say the least of it, cannot be familiar to both parties. On one side, therefore, nothing farther remains to be said; for, however lovely the egotist may be in her own person, no man, or woman either, is prepared to have her substituted for the world in general, though it seems more than probable that the individual herself might not object to such a transposition.

It is difficult to decide, whether the annoyance arising from maternal eloquence, should be placed before or after that arising from the prevalence of self in conversation; but certainly there are many who can speak feelingly, of the never-ending penance they have to endure from the partial views, and warm feelings of injudicious mothers, leading them out into a series of comments and commendations, as interminable as the freaks and supposed eccentricities of their own little cherubs, in whose flaxen hair, and chubby faces, the beholder sees nothing to distinguish them from other children. Yet such are the features presented to the eye of the fond mother, that she believes no infant eye looked or lisped so sweetly as her own And, happy is it for her that a kind Providence has implanted in her bosom this conviction. We would only whisper in her ear, that there are others to whom the case admits of doubt; and while they have too much kind feeling to wish to undeceive her, she ought at least to spare them the persecution, in which, by their silent acquiescence, they are sometimes involved.

Another class of annoying talkers, whose claims to eminence in this line I am in no way disposed to contest, consists of the talkers of mere common-place—those who say nothing, but what we could have said ourselves, had we deemed it worth our while, and who never on any occasion, or by any chance, give utterance to a new idea. Such people will talk. They seem to consider it their especial duty to talk, and no symptoms of inattention in their hearers, no impatient answer nor averted ear, nor even the interminable monotony of their own prattle, has the power to hush them into silence. If they fail in one thing, they try another; but, unfortunately for them, there is a transmuting medium in their own discourse, that would turn to dust the golden opinions of the wisest of men.

We naturally ask in what consists that objectionable common-place of which we complain, since the tenor of their conversation is not unlike the conversation of others. It is in reality too like, too much composed of the fillings-up of conversation in general. It has nothing distinctive in it, and, like certain letters we have seen, would answer the purpose as well, if addressed to one individual as another.

The talker of common-place is always interested in the weather, which forms an all-sufficient resource when other subjects fail. One would think, from the frequency with which the individual remarks upon the rising of clouds, and the falling of rain, she was perpetually on the point of setting out on a journey. But she treats the seasons with the same respect, and loses no opportunity of telling the farmer who is silently suffering from a wet harvest, that the autumn has been unusually unpropitious. If you cough, she hopes you have not taken cold, but really colds are extremely prevalent. If you bring out your work, she admires both your industry and your taste, and assures you that rich colours are well thrown off by a dark ground. If books are the subject of conservation, she inquires whether you have read one that has just had a twelvemonth's run of popularity. She thinks that authors sometimes go a little too far, but concludes with what appears in her opinion to be a universal case, that much may be said on both sides. From books she proceeds to authors; expatiates upon the imagination of Shakspeare, and the strength of mind possessed by Hannah More; and deliberately inquires whether you do not agree with her in her sentiments respecting both. Nay, so far does reality exceed imagination, that I once heard a very sweet and amiable woman, whose desire to be at the same time both edifying and agreeable, somewhat outran her originality of thought, exclaim, in one of those pauses incident to conversation—"What an excellent book the Bible is! " Now, there is no gainsaying such an assertion, and it is almost equally impossible to assent. Conversation, therefore, always flags where common-place exists, because it elicits nothing, touches no answering chord, nor conveys any other idea than that of bare sound, to the ear of the reluctant listener.

Another and most prolific source of annoyance is found amongst that class of persons who choose to converse on subjects interesting to themselves, without regard to time, or place, or general appropriateness. Whatever they take up, either as their ruling topic, or as one of momentary interest, is forced upon society, whether in season or out of season; and they often feel surprised and mortified that their favourite subjects, in themselves not unfrequently well chosen, are received by others with so cold a welcome. How many worthy individuals, whose minds are richly stored, and whose laudable desire is to disseminate useful knowledge, entirely defeat their own ends by this want of adaptation; and many, whose conversation might be both amusing and instructive, from this cause seldom meet with a patient hearer.

Old people are peculiarly liable to this error; and it would be well to provide against the garrulity and wearisomeness of advanced age, by cultivating such powers of discrimination as would enable us habitually to discover what is acceptable, or otherwise, in conversation.

It occasionally happens that the mistress of a house, the kind hospitable mistress, who has been at a world of pains to make every body comfortable, is the very last person at the table, beside whom any of her guests would desire to be placed; because they know, that being once linked in with her interminable chain of prattle, they will have no chance of escape until the ladies rise to withdraw; and there are few who would not prefer quietly partaking of her soups and sauces, to hearing them described. Women of this description, having tired out every body at home, and taught every ear to turn away, are voracious of attention when they can command it, or even that appearance of it which the visiter politely puts on. Charmed with the novelty of her situation in having caught a hearer, she makes the most of him. Warming with her subject, and describing still more copiously, she looks into his face with an expression bordering on ecstasy; and were it not that she considerately spares him the task of a rejoinder, his situation would be as intolerable as the common routine of table-talk could make it.

In about the same class of agreeables with this good lady, might be placed the profuse teller of tales, whose natural flow of language and fertility of ideas lead her so far away from the original story, that neither the narrator nor the listener would be able to answer, if suddenly inquired of—what the story was about. This is a very common fault amongst female talkers, whose versatility of mind and sensibility of feeling, render them peculiarly liable to be diverted from any definite object. It is only wonderful that the same quickness of apprehension does not teach them the impossibility of obtaining hearers on such terms.

Nor must we forget, amongst the abuses of conversation, the random talkers, —those who talk from impulse only, and rush upon you with what- ever happens to be uppermost in their own minds, or most pleasing to their fancy at the time, without waiting to ascertain whether the individual they address is sad or merry, —at liberty to listen, or preoccupied with some weightier and more interesting subject.

Whatever the topic of conversation, thus obtruded upon society, may be, it is evident there must be a native obtuseness and vulgarity in the mind of the individual who thus offends, or she would wait before she spoke, to tune her voice to some degree of harmony with the feelings of those around her.

Thus far we have noticed only the trifling abuses of conversation, and of such we have, perhaps already, had more than enough; though the catalogue might easily be continued through as many volumes as it occupies pages here. There are other aspects more serious, under which the abuse of conversation must be contemplated; and the first of these is—as it relates to carelessness or design in exercising its power to give pain.

It is difficult to conceive that a deliberate desire to give pain could exist in any but the most malignant bosom; but habitual want of regard to what is painful to others, may easily be the cause of inflicting upon them real misery.

We have all observed—perhaps some of us felt, the sting of a taunting or an ill-timed jest; and never is the suffering it occasions, or the effect it produces, so much to be regretted, as when it wrings sharp tears from the gentle eyes of childhood. Ye know not what ye do—might well be said to those who thus burn up the blossoms of youth, and send back the fresh, warm current of feeling, to stagnate at the heart.

It would be impossible, even if such were our object, always to discover exactly when we did give pain; but surely it would be a study well worthy of a benevolent and enlightened mind, to ascertain the fact, with as much precision as we are capable of. What, for instance, do we feel on being called upon to sympathize with a young lady, who is at the same moment pointed out to us as one whose father a short time before had put an end to his existence, when the recollection simultaneously flashes upon us, that during the whole of the past evening, we engaged the attention of the very same young lady with a detailed account of the melancholy scenes we had sometimes witnessed in an insane asylum? Yet, neither the pain inflicted by such conversation is greater, nor is its carelessness more culpable in us, than is that of a large portion of the ill- judged, random speeches we give utterance to every day.

Nor is it in common conversation that carelessness of giving pain is felt, so much as in the necessary duties of advising and finding fault. I am inclined to think no very agreeable way of telling people of their faults has ever yet been discovered; but certainly there is a difference, as great as that which separates light from darkness, between reproof judiciously and injudiciously administered. By carelessness in not regulating our tones, and looks, and manner, when reproving others, we may convey either too much, or too little meaning, and thus defeat our own purposes; we may even convey an impression the exact opposite of that designed, and awaken feelings of bitterness, revenge, and malignity, in the mind of the individual we are solicitous to serve.

Let no one therefore presume to do good, either by instruction or advice, unless they have learned something of the human heart. It may appear, on the first view of the subject, a difficult and arduous study, but it is one that never can be begun too early or pursued too long. It is one also, in the pursuit of which women never need despair, as they possess the universal key of sympathy, by which all hearts may be unlocked, — some, it is true, with considerable difficulty, and some but partially at last; yet, if the key be applied by a delicate and skilful hand, there is little doubt but some measure of success will reward the endeavour.

We have said before, and we again repeat, it is scarcely possible to believe that beings constituted as women are—kindly affectioned, and tenderly susceptible of pain themselves—should be capable of wantonly and designedly inflicting pain upon others. Nature revolts from the thought. We look at the smile of beauty, and exclaim, "Impossible! " We pursue the benevolent visitant of the sick in her errands of mercy, and say, "It cannot be. " Yet, after all, we fear it must be charged upon the female sex, that they do assist occasionally in the circulation of petty scandal, and that it is not always from carelessness that they let slip the envenomed shaft, or speak daggers where they dare not use them. Nor are the speakers alone to blame. The hearers ought at least to participate, for if the habit of depreciating character were discountenanced in society, it would soon cease to exist, or exist only in occasional attempts, to be defeated as soon as made.

Few women have the hardihood to confess that they delight in this kind of conversation. But let the experiment be made in mixed society, of course not under the influence of true religious feeling, though perhaps the party might be such as would feel a little scandalized at being told they were not. Let a clever and sarcastic woman take the field, not, professedly, to talk against her neighbours on her own authority, but to throw in the hearsay of the day, by way of spice to the general conversation; giving to a public man, his private stigma—to an author, his unsaleable book—to the rich man, his trading ancestry—to the poor, his unquestionable imprudence—to the beau, his borrowed plumes, —and to the belle, her artificial bloom. We grant that this mass of poisoning matter thrown in at once, would be likely to offend the taste. It must therefore be skilfully proportioned, distributed with nice distinction, and dressed up with care. Will there not then be a large proportion of attentive listeners gathered round the speaker, smiling a ready assent to what they had themselves not dared to utter, and nodding, as if in silent recognition of some fact they had previously been made acquainted with in a more private way?

Now all this while there may be seated in another part of the room, a person whose sole businless is to tell the good she knows, believes, or has heard of others. She is not a mere relater of facts, but equally talented, shrewd, and discriminating with the opposite party, only she is restricted to the detail of what is good. I simply ask, for I wish not to pursue the subject farther, Which of these talkers will be likely to obtain the largest group of listeners?

It is not, after all, by any consistent or determined attack upon character, that so much mischief is done, as by interlarding otherwise agreeable conversation with the sly hope of pretended charity—that certain things are not as they have been reported; or the kind wish—that apparent merit was real, or might last.

English society is so happily constituted, that women have little temptation to any open vice. They must lose all respect for themselves, before they would venture so far to forget their respectability. But they have temptations as powerful to them, as open vice to others; and not the less so, for being insidious. Who would believe that the passions of envy, hatred, and revenge could lurk within the gentle bosom over which those folds of dove-coloured drapery are falling? The lady has been prevailed upon to sing for the amusement of the company. Blushing and hesitating, she is just about to be led to the place of exhibition, when another movement, in a distant part of the room, where her own advance was not observed, has placed upon the seat of honour, a younger, and perhaps more lovely woman; and she lays open the very piece of music which the lady in the dovelike colour had believed herself the only person present who could sing. The musician charms the company. The next day, our dove hears of nothing but this exquisite performance; and at last she is provoked to say, "No wonder she plays so well, for I understand she does nothing else. Her mamma was ill the other day with a dreadful headach, and she played on, the whole afternoon, because she was going to a party in the evening, and wished to keep herself in practice. "

Now, there is little in this single speech. It is almost too trifling for remark; but it may serve as a specimen of thousands, which are no determined falsehoods, nay, possibly, no falsehoods at all, and yet originate in feelings as diametrically opposed to christian meekness, love, and charity, as are the malignant passions of envy, hatred, and revenge.

I must again repeat, that I know the evil exists not in this individual act, but in the state of the heart where it originates; yet I write thus earnestly about seeming trifles, because I believe few young persons are sufficiently alive to their importance; because I know that the minor morals of domestic life exercise a vital influence over the well-being of society; and because the peace of whole families is sometimes destroyed, by the outward observance of religious duty not being supported by an equally strenuous observance of these delicate but essential points.

In studying the art, or rather the duty of being agreeable—a duty which all kindly-disposed persons will be anxious to observe—it is of importance to inquire, from whence originate the errors here specified, with the long catalogue that might follow in their train? So far as they are confined to misapprehension of what is really agreeable, they may be said to originate in the innate selfishness of our nature gaining the mastery over our judgment; beyond this, they originate in the evil propensities of the human heart, which, when the influence of popular feeling operates against their exhibition in any gross and palpable form, infuse themselves, as it were, into the very current of our existence, and poison all our secret springs of feeling.

In order to correct the former, it is necessary that the judgment should be awakened. But as habits of selfishness, long indulged, involve the understanding in a cloud too dense to be altogether dispelled, it is the more important that youth should be so trained as to acquire habits of constant and unremitting mental reference to the feelings and characters of others; so that a quickness of perception, almost like intuitive knowledge, shall enable them to carry out the kindly purposes they are taught to cherish, into the delicate and minute affairs of life, and thus render them the means not only of giving pleasure, but of warding off pain.

It may appear a harsh conclusion to come to, that the little errors of conversation to which allusion has been made, and which are often conspicuous in what are called good sort of people, really owe their existence to selfishness; but it should be remembered, that to this assertion the writer is far from adding, that those who act with more tact, and avoid such errors, are necessarily free from the same fault. There may be a refined as well as a gross selfishness, and both may be equal in their intensity and power.

But let us go back to the cases already specified. If the artist were not habitually more intent upon his own gratification, than upon that of his companions, he would keep his hobby in the back- ground, and allow himself time to perceive that the attention of his companion was pre-occupied by subjects more agreeable to him. The same may certainly be said of the more common fault of making self the ruling topic of conversation; and this applies with equal truth to self-depreciation, as to self-praise.

The case is too clear and simple to need farther argument. It must be the habit of acting from that first and most powerful impulse of our nature, and just pouring forth the fulness of our own hearts, discharging our own imagination of its load, and emptying the storehouse of our own memory, without regard to fitness or preparation in the soil upon which the seed may fall, or the harvest it is likely to produce, that renders conversation sometimes tasteless and vapid, and sometimes inexpressibly annoying.

The weightier responsibilities which attach to the talent of conversation, do not appear to fall directly within the compass of a work expressly devoted to the morals of domestic life. It is, however, a fact of great importance to establish, that a woman's private conversation—for in public they converse too much alike—is the surest evidence of her mind being imbued, or not imbued with just and religious principles; that where it is uniformly trifling, there can be no predominating desire to promote the interests of religion in the world; and where, on the other hand, it is uniformly solemn and sedate, it is ill calculated to recommend the course it would advocate with effect; that where it abounds in sarcasm, invective, and abuse even of what is evil, it never emanates from a mind in perfect unison with what is good; and that, where it is always smooth, and sweet, and complacent, it must be deficient in one of the grand uses of conversation—its correction and reproof: finally, that where it is carried on in public or in private, without the least desire to elicit truth, to correct mistakes in relation or opinion, to establish principle, to disseminate useful knowledge, to warn of danger, or to perform that most difficult, but most important of all duties—to correct the faults of friends—there must be something wrong at the heart's core, from whence this waste of words is flowing; and sad will be the final account, if, for each day of a lengthened existence upon earth, this great engine of moral good and evil has been thus performing its fruitless labour—for time, without an object; for eternity, without reward.

CHAPTER VI. CONVERSATION.

IT may appear somewhat paradoxical to commence a CHAPTER on the uses of conversation, by pointing out the uses of being silent; yet such is the importance to a woman, of knowing exactly when to cease from conversation, and when to withhold it altogether, that the silence of the female sex seems to have become proverbially synonymous with a degree of merit almost too great to be believed in as a fact. There could be no agreeable conversation carried on, if there were no good listeners; and from her position in society, it is the peculiar province of a woman, rather to lead others out into animated and intelligent communication, than to be intent upon making communications from the resources of her own mind.

Besides this, there are times when men, especially if they are of moody temperament, are more offended and annoyed by being talked to, than they could be by the greatest personal affront from the same quarter; and a woman of taste will readily detect the forbidding frown, the close-shut lips, and the averted eye, which indicate a determination not to be drawn out. She will then find opportunity for the indulgence of those secret trains of thought and feeling which naturally arise in every human mind; and while she plies her busy needle, and sits quietly musing by the side of her husband, her father, or her brother, she may be adding fresh materials from the world of thought, to that fund of conversational amusement, which she is ever ready to bring forward for their use.

By the art of conversation, therefore, as I am about to treat the subject in the present CHAPTER, I would by no means be understood to mean the mere act of talking, but that cultivation and exercise of the conversational powers which is most conducive to social enjoyment, and most productive of beneficial influence upon our fellow-creatures.

I have already asserted of conversation, that it is a fruitful source of human happiness and misery, a powerful engine of moral good and evil; and few, I should suppose, would deny the truth of this assertion. Yet, notwithstanding the preva- lence of this conviction, the art of conversation is seldom or never cultivated as a branch of modern education. It is true, the youthful mind is stimulated into early and immature expansion; and the youthful memory is stored with facts; but the young student, released from the trammels of school discipline, is thrown upon society in a state of total ignorance of the means of imparting her knowledge so as to render it available in raising the general tone of conversation; and the consequence mostly is, she is so engrossed by the new life into which she is suddenly introduced, and so occupied in learning what must be acquired before she can make any respectable figure in what is called society, that she closes the door upon the storehouse she has spent so many years of her life in filling; and finding little use for the materials accumulated there, is only known in after years to have had a good education, by hearing her occasionally exclaim—"I learned all about that at school, but have entirely forgotten it since. "

The English woman, whose peculiar part it is to blend all that is productive of benefit in her intellectual powers, with all that is conducive to happiness in her affections, would do well to give her attention as early as possible to the uses of conversation; and if a system could be formed for teaching some of the simple rules of conversation as an art, it would be found more advantageous to women in their social capacity, than many of the branches of learning which they now spend years in acquiring.

To converse by rule has indeed a startling sound, and few, we are apt to conclude, on a slight consideration of the subject, would recommend themselves by such a process. The same conclusion, however, is always rushed upon by the young genius who first begins to try her skill in the sister arts of painting and poetry. Yet, in proceeding, she finds at every step, that there must be a rule, a plan, a system, or that genius, with all her profusion of materials, will be unable to form them into such a whole as will afford pleasure even to the most uninitiated.

I am aware I incur some risk of being charged both with ignorance and enthusiasm, when I express my belief that the art of conversation might in some measure be reduced to a system, taught in our schools, and rendered an important part of female education; but I am not aware that my belief can be proved to be ill-founded, until the experiment has been fairly tried.

Let an individual who has never heard of botany, go forth into one of our English meadows in the month of June, and gaze upon the luxuriance of flowers, and leaves, and shooting stems, which there would meet his eye. Tell him that all these distinct and separate plants have been classed, and resolved into their appropriate orders, and he will exclaim, "Impossible! it cannot be. "

I must allow that the case is not, strictly speaking, a similar one. There are difficulties of no trifling magnitude in reducing the faculties of the human mind to any thing like order, and in laying down rules for the promotion of human happiness, except on the broad scale of moral philosophy. But let the two cases be fairly tried, and I am still unconvinced that the most apparently impracticable would not be attended with a measure of success.

If we consider the number of books that have been written on the subject of botany, the number of lectures that have been delivered, the number of years it has been taught, and the number of wise men who have made it their chief study: and if in comparison with a subject upon which such vast machinery of mind has been brought to operate, we do but mention that of Conversation, to which no one entire volume has, perhaps, ever yet been devoted, a smile of derision will most probably be the only notice our observation will excite.

I would not be understood to speak lightly of a knowledge of botany, or to depreciate the value of any other science. All I would maintain is this, that to know every thing that can be known in art and nature, is of little value to a woman, if she has not at the same time learned to communicate her knowledge in such a manner as to render it agreeable and serviceable to others.

A woman does not converse more agreeably, because she is able to define botanically the difference between a rose and a buttercup, though it may be desirable to be able to do so when asked; but because she has a quick insight into character, has tact to select the subjects of conversation best suited to her auditors, and to pursue them just so long as they excite interest, and engage attention.

With regard to the art of conversation, therefore, adaptation may be laid down as the primary rule—vivacity, or rather freshness, as the second—and the establishment of a fact, or the deduction of a moral, as the third.

Why should not the leisure hours at school be filled up by the practice of these rules, not only as a recreation, but as a pleasing art, in which it would be much to the advantage of every woman to excel? Why should not the mistress of the school devote her time occasionally to the exercise of this art in the midst of her pupils, who might by her winning manners be invited in their turn to practise upon her? And why should not some plan be invented for encouraging the same exercise amongst the junior members of the establishment? Each girl, for instance, might be appointed for a day or a week, the converser with, or entertainer of, one of her fellow-students, taking all in rotation; so that in their hours of leisure, it should be her business to devote herself to her companion, as it is that of a host to a guest. A report should then be given in at the expiration of the day or week, by the girl whose part it was to be conversed with, and by encouraging her to state whether she has been annoyed or interested, wearied or amused, in the presence of her companion, who should in her turn have the liberty of commending or complaining of her, as an attentive or inattentive listener, a good or bad responder, such habits of candour and sincerity would be cultivated, as are of essential service in the formation of the moral character.

The practice of this art, as here recommended, would not necessarily be restricted in its operation to any particular number. Those who attained the greatest proficiency might extend their con- versational powers to other members of the establishment; and thus might be constituted little amicable societies, in which all the faculties most likely to recommend the young students in their future association with the world, would be called into exercise, and rendered conducive to the general good.

To the class of women chiefly referred to in this work, it is perhaps most important that they should be able to converse with interest and effect. A large portion of their time is spent in the useful labour of the needle, an occupation which of all others requires something to vary its monotony, and render less irksome its seemingly interminable duration; they are frequently employed in nursing the sick, when appropriate and well-timed conversation may occasionally beguile the sufferer into forgetfulness of pain; and they are also much at home—at their humble, quiet homes, where excitement from extraneous causes seldom comes, and where, if they are unacquainted with the art, and uninitiated in the practice of conversation, their days are indeed heavy, and their evenings worse than dull.

The women of England are not only peculiarly in need of this delightful relaxation to blend with their daily cares; but, until the late rapid increase of superficial refinement, they were adapted, by their habits and mode of life, for cultivating their conversational powers in a very high degree. Their time was not occupied by the artificial embellishments of polished life, they were thrown directly upon their own resources for substantial comfort, and thus they acquired a foundation of character which rendered their conversation sensible, original, and full of point. It is greatly to be apprehended that the increased facilities for imparting instruction in the present day, have not produced a proportionate increase in the facilities of conversing; and it is well worthy the attention of those who give their time and thoughts to the invention of improved means of disseminating knowledge, to inquire what is the best method of doing this by conversation, as well as by books.

It is not, however, strictly speaking, in imparting a knowledge of general facts, that the highest use of conversation consists. General facts may be recorded in books, and books may be circulated to the remotest range of civilized society; but there are delicate touches of feeling too evanescent to bear the impress of any tangible character; there are mental and spiritual appliances, that must be immediate to be available; and who has not known the time when they would have given the wealth of worlds for the power to unburden their full hearts before the moment of acceptance should be gone, or the attentive ear be closed for ever?

The difficulty is seldom so great in knowing what ought to be said, as in knowing how to speak, what mode of expression would be most acceptable, or what turn the conversation ought to take, so as best to introduce the point in question.

Nor is the management of the voice an unimportant branch of this art. There are never-to-be-forgotten tones, with which some cruel word has been accompanied, that have impressed themselves upon every heart; and there are also tones of kindness equally indelible, which had, perhaps, more influence at the time they were heard, than the language they were employed to convey. "It was not what she said, but the tone of voice in which she spoke, " is the complaint of many a wounded spirit; and welcome and soothing to the listening ear, is every tone that tells of hope and gladness.

There is scarcely any source of enjoyment more immediately connected at once with the heart and with the mind, than that of listening to a sensible and amiable woman when she converses in a melodious and well-regulated voice, when her language and pronunciation are easy and correct, and when she knows how to adapt her conversation to the characters and habits of those around her.

Women, considered in their distinct and abstract nature, as isolated beings, must lose more than half their worth. They are, in fact, from their own constitution, and from the station they occupy in the world, strictly speaking, relative creatures. If, therefore, they are endowed only with such faculties as render them striking and distinguished in themselves, without the faculty of instrumentality, they are only as dead letters in the volume of human life, filling what would otherwise be a blank space, but doing nothing more.

All the knowledge in the world, therefore, without an easy and felicitous method of conveying it to others, would be but a profitless possession to a woman; while a very inferior portion of knowledge, with this method, might render her an interesting and delightful companion.

None need despair, then, if shut out by homely avocations, by straitened means, or by other unavoidable causes, from learning all the lessons taught at school; for there are lessons to be learned at home, around the domestic hearth, and even in the obscurity of rural life, perhaps of more importance in the summing-up of human happiness.

One of the popular uses of conversation is, to pass away time without being conscious of its duration; and, unworthy as this object unquestionably is, the fact that conversation is employed more than any other means for such a purpose, is a convincing proof of its importance and its power.

It is so natural to converse, that one of the severest punishments inflicted upon degraded human nature, is that of being denied the liberty of speech. How desirable is it, then, that what is done every hour in all classes of society, and under almost every variety of circumstance, should be done for some good purpose, and done in the best possible manner!

To converse well in company, is a point of ambition with many women, and few are insensible to the homage paid by the most sincere of all flatterers—a group of attentive listeners. So far as this talent enables a woman of elevated mind to give a higher tone to conversation in general, it is indeed a valuable gift; but that of being able to converse in an agreeable and appro- priate manner in a sick-room, with an aged parent or distressed relative, or with a friend in delicate and trying circumstances, is a gift of far higher and more ennobling character.

I have already remarked, that attendance upon the sick is one of the most frequent and familiar, at the same time that it is one of the most sacred of the duties devolving upon the class of women here described. It is much, to be able gently and skilfully to smooth the pillow for the aching head, to administer the cordial draught, to guide the feeble steps, and to watch through the sleepless and protracted hours of night. But these are services rendered only to the suffering body. The mind—the unextinguishable mind, may all the while be sorely in need of the oil with which its waning lamp should still be trimmed. And how shall this be administered? The practised nurses hired for the occasion make rude and ill-advised attempts to raise the drooping spirits of the patient by their vulgar pleasantry; books are too wearisome, and tell only of far-off and by-gone things, when the whole interest of the sufferer is concentrated into the present moment, and fixed upon himself.

It happens more frequently and more happily amongst the middle classes in England, that nurses and domestics cannot well be hired, and that the chief attention required by the patient, devolves upon the females of the family. How differently in this case is the sufferer dealt with! There is no appearance of coming in expressly to converse with him; but while a gentle and kind-hearted woman steals with noiseless tread about the room, arranging every article of comfort, and giving to the whole apartment an air of refreshment or repose, she is watching every indication of an opening for conversation, that may beguile the lingering hours of their tediousness, and lead the sufferer to forget his pain. There are moments, even in seasons of sickness, when a little well-timed pleasantry is far from being unacceptable. She watches for these, and turns them to account, by going just so far in her playfulness, as the exhausted frame can bear without injury. When sympathy is called for, as it is on such occasions almost unceasingly, she yields it freely and fully, though not to any prolonged extent, as regards the case immediately under her care; but continuing the same tone and manner, and with evidently the same feeling, she speaks of other cases of suffering, of some friend or neighbour; and the more recent and immediate the instances, the more likely they will be to divert the mind of the patient from himself. These of course are not brought forward with anything like a taunting insinuation that the patient is not worse than others, but simply as if her own mind was full of the impressions they are calculated to excite; and by these means, suiting her voice and her countenance to the facts she is relating, she invests them with an interest which even to the selfish invalid is irresistible.

Varying with every change in the temper and mood of the patient, her conversation assumes every variety that is calculated to please, always subdued and kept under by such delicate touches of feeling, such intense watchfulness, and such lively sensibility, that the faintest shadow cannot pass across the aching brow, nor the slightest indication of a smile across the lips, but it serves as an index for her either to change the subject of her discourse, to be silent, or to proceed. There is along with all this a kindness in her voice which no pen was ever so eloquent as to describe; and there are moments of appealing weakness on the part of the invalid, when she pours forth the full tide of her affection, in language that prosperity and health would never have taught her how to use.

Beyond these seasons of intercourse, however, and of far deeper value, are those in which the burdened soul of him who feels himself to be fast hastening to the confines of eternity, will sometimes seek a human ear for the utterance of its anxieties and fears, and appeal to a human heart for counsel in its hours of need. It may be that the individual has never been accustomed to converse on these subjects—knows not how to begin—and is ashamed to condemn, as he feels that he must do, the whole of his past life. Who then, but the friend who has been near him in all his recent humiliations and trials, who has shared them both to her very utmost, and thus obtained his confidence, —who but his patient and untiring nurse, can mark and understand the struggle of his feelings, and lead them forth by partial anticipations, so gently that he is neither pained nor humbled by the whole confession.

Perchance it is at the hour of midnight, when fever gives him strength, and darkness hides his countenance, and he hears the sweet tones of that encouraging voice, now modulated to the expression of a sympathy the most intense, and a love that many waters could not quench. There is no surprise in her rejoinder, when at last his lips have spoken what he could not utter by the light of day, but a few simple words, more like those of recognition of what she had known before, and of what it is the lot of many to experience; and then, if ever, is the golden moment when the power to speak without wounding, and yet to speak home, is indeed an inestimable gift.

It is true that suitable and salutary words might be written out for some such occasion; but so differently constituted are human minds, that the same words would scarcely prove suitable and salutary to any two individuals, out of the countless myriads who throng the peopled earth.

Nor is the chamber of sickness the only situation in which the power of conversing easily and appropriately is of inestimable value. There are other cases of trial, of suffering, and of anxious solicitude, in which the mind would prey upon itself, even to the injury of the bodily frame, if not diverted from its object, and beguiled by pleasant conversation.

In seasons of protracted endurance, when some anticipated crisis, of immeasurable good or evil, comes not at the expected time, and every fresh disappointment only adds to the feverish restlessness which no human constitution is strong enough to sustain unharmed; what amusement could be devised for such a time, at all comparable to interesting and judicious conversation, gently touching upon the exciting theme, and then leading off by some of those innumerable channels which woman's ingenuity is so quick to discover, and so apt to make use of for purposes of generosity and kindness?

There are fireside scenes, too, of frequent and familiar occurrence, in which this feminine faculty may be rendered more serviceable than all other accomplishments—scenes that derive not their sadness from acute or lively suffering, but are yet characterized by an inexpressible kind of melancholy, arising from the moodiness of man, or the perverseness of woman, or, perhaps, from a combination of domestic disagreeables attaching to every member of the family, and forming over their better feelings a sort of incrustation, that must be dissolved or broken through, before anything like cheerfulness can shine forth.

There is, perhaps, more real sadness arising from causes like this, than from the more definite misfortunes with which we are visited; and not sadness only, but a kind of resentment bordering on secret malignity, as if each member of the family had poisoned the happiness of the others; and looks are directed askance, books are opened, and their leaves are methodically folded over; and yet the long dull evening will not wear away.

How like a ministering angel then is the woman, who, looking off from her work, directs her conversation to that member of the family who appears most accessible, and, having gained his attention, gives the subject such a turn as to draw in the attention of another, and perhaps a third, until all at last, without being aware of it, have joined in conversing on the same topic, and the close of the evening finds them mutually agreeable to each other. On such occasions it is by no means an insignificant attainment to be able to awaken a laugh, for if two or three can be brought to laugh together, the incrustation is effectually broken, and they will be good friends without farther effort.

I know it would be fruitless to lay down any minute and specific rules for conversation, because none could be acted upon safely without strict reference to the object upon which they might be brought to bear. Yet it may be said to be a rule almost without exception, that all persons are pleased to be talked to about themselves, their own affairs, and their own connexions, provided only it is done with judgment, delicacy, and tact. When all other topics have been tried without effect, this will seldom be found to fail. Not, certainly, pursued upon what is described as the American plan, of decided inquisitiveness, but by remote allusions, and frequent recurrence to what has already been drawn forth, making it the foundation for greater confidence, and more definite communication.

That species of universal politeness, which prompts inquiry after the relations of the stranger or the guest, appears to be founded upon this principle, occurring, as it so frequently does, where there can be no possible interest on the part of the inquirer.

It it not, however, for the purpose of pretending to that which does not really exist, that conversation can be recommended as an art, but simply for facilitating the expression of feelings which could not be so well explained by a more direct assurance of their nature and existence.

When a stranger from a distance—perhaps an orphan, or one who is compelled by adverse circumstances to seek the means of pecuniary support—comes to take up her abode in a family, no member of which she has ever seen before, by what means can the mother or the mistress of it make her feel that she is at home? she may tell her in plain words that she is disposed to make her comfortable, but it will touch with infinitely more force the heart of the stranger, if, with a countenance of kindly interest, she makes frequent and delicate mention of her friends, of her brothers or sisters, or other near relations, or even of the part of the world in which she has been accustomed to reside. This kind of mention, frequently bestowed with gentleness, and evident regard to the facts it elicits or the confidence it draws forth, will be much more effectual in gaining the desired end, than the warmest expressions of affectionate solicitude for the stranger herself.

I know that conversation, simply studied as an art, without right motives for its exercise, will be found of little benefit, either to society, or to the individuals who practise it. All I would maintain is, that it may be made the medium of conferring happiness—the instrument of doing good—and that to a greater extent than any other accomplishment in which woman can excel. For want of facility in speaking appropriately, how much good feeling is lost to the world, buried in the bosom where it originates, and where it becomes a burden and a load, from the very consciousness of inability to make it understood and felt.

How often do we hear the bitterest lamentations to this effect—"If I could but have told her what I felt—if I could but have addressed her appropriately at the time—if I had but known how to make the conversation lead to the point—but now the time has passed, and I may never have so suitable an opportunity again. "

Besides the cases already described, there are some darker passages in human life, when women are thrown upon the actual charm of their conversation, for rendering more alluring, the home that is not valued as it should be. Perhaps a husband has learned before his marriage the fatal habit of seeking recreation in scenes of excitement and convivial mirth. It is but natural that such habits should with difficulty be broken off, and that he should look with something like weariness upon the quiet and monotony of his own fireside. Music cannot always please, and books to such a man are a tasteless substitute for the evening party. He may possibly admire his wife, consider her extremely good-looking, and, for a woman, think her very pleasant; but the sobriety of matrimony palls upon his vitiated taste, and he longs to feel himself a free man again amongst his old associates.

Nothing would disgust this man so much, or drive him away so effectually, as any assumption on the part of his wife, of a right to detain him. The next most injudicious thing she could do, would be to exhibit symptoms of grief—of real sorrow and distress at his leaving her; for whatever may be said in novels on the subject of beauty in tears, seems to be rendered null and void by the circumstance of marriage having taken place between the parties.

The rational woman, whose conversation on this occasion is to serve her purpose more effectually than tears, knows better than to speak of what her husband would probably consider a most unreasonable subject of complaint. She tries to recollect some incident, some trait of character, or some anecdote of what has lately occurred within her knowledge, and relates it in her most lively and piquant manner. If conscious of beauty, she tries a little raillery, and plays gently upon some of her husband's not unpleasing peculiarities, looking all the while as disengaged and unsuspecting as she can. If his attention becomes fixed, she gives her conversation a more serious turn, and plunges at once into some theme of deep and absorbing interest. If her companion grows restless, she changes the subject, and again recollects something laughable to relate to him. Yet all the while her own poor heart is aching with the feverish anxiety that vacillates between the extremes of hope and fear. She gains courage, however, as time steals on, for her husband is by her side, and with her increasing courage her spirits become exhilarated, and she is indeed the happy woman she has hitherto but appeared; for at last her husband looks at his watch, is astonished to find it is too late to join his friends; and while the evening closes in, he wonders whether any other man has a wife so delightful and entertaining as his own.

Again, there is a class of beings, unfortunately for themselves, not always welcomed into good society, and yet severely blamed for seeking bad—a nondescript species of humanity, not properly called boys, nor worthily called men, who are, above all other creatures, the most difficult to converse with. They seem, in fact, to be discarded from society, for old women are afraid of them, while young ones pronounce them bores; and old men seem uniformly inclined to put them down, while young ones do little to raise them up. Yet in these very individuals, during this season of incipient manhood, the character of the future statesman or citizen, father or friend, is undergoing the process of formation; and all the while the step that owes half its fleetness to the hope of leaving care and sorrow in the distance, bounds on with triumphant recklessness, because there is no friendly voice to arrest its progress, or direct its course.

Who takes the trouble to converse with a youth of this description, for we confess it is a trouble, except where personal affection prompts the act? Is there not one who will kindly endeavour to make the young heart confess itself, for a heart there must be under all this rude and turbulent exterior? Yes, there is one. The reckless boy, after receiving a thousand insults, after having been elbowed off by one, pushed away by a second, and made game of by a third, comes home to his mother, and finds that his own fireside is indeed the happiest place on earth to him. His mother does what no one else will condescend to do—she converses with him—she treats him like a rational being. Interested in his amusements because they are his, she talks to him about his sports, his companions, and all the minutiæ that fill up his daily life, anticipating all the while such feelings and sentiments as she believes him to possess, or at least gives him credit for, and thus leads him to confess. While the boy, feeling within himself the dawning of a brighter epoch in his existence, the stirring of half-formed thoughts about to be matured, is happy and grateful to be thus encouraged to speak freely, and to be his better self.

Of evenings spent in this manner, who shall estimate the value, remembered as they often are in after life, and blended as they safely may be with that portion of self-respect which is always found to support the persevering, the upright, and the truly great?

The cases already mentioned, serve but as specimens of the mass of evidence that might be brought forward in favour of the utility of conversation judiciously carried on; what then must be said of the responsibility of those who possess this talent in its highest perfection, and either neglect to use it for any laudable purpose, or devote it to a bad one?

It seems to be too much the opinion of people in general, that agreeable conversation, like many other agreeable things, is only to be used for the benefit of guests and strangers. The truly English, domestic, and fireside companion has a higher estimate of this talent. She knows little of what is called the world, and would be too diffident to attempt to make a figure in it if she did. Her world is her home, and here, on days of laborious duty, as well as on days of pleasure, when the family circle are met around their homely hearth, as well as when the distinguished guest is with them, it is her chief delight to beguile, what might otherwise be to them, heavy hours, with cheerful conversation. It is to her parents, her husband, her brothers, and her sisters, as well as to her intimate friends, that she is the entertaining and instructive companion, adapting herself to their different moods and temperaments, leading forth their thoughts beyond themselves, and raising them above the sordid and vexatious cares of every-day existence, until her voice becomes the music of her home, and her presence the charm that unites the different members of her household in a sacred bond of fellowship and peace.

The power of conversing well, presents a great temptation to a vain woman to use it for the gratification of her self-complacency. As there are few of the minor circumstances of life more mortifying than to find, that when you speak, no one listens to the end of your story or remark; so, there is no kind of flattery more irresistible than to find that your conversation gathers hearers, more and more; and women are but too quick to detect the interest they excite depicted upon every face.

There is, however, a wide difference between the moral state of the woman who converses well in company, solely for the sake of obtaining admiration, and of her who converses well for the sake of making the time pass pleasantly or profitably to others. The former will be sure to be found amongst the gentlemen, especially if she be pleasing in her appearance, and she will have wholly overlooked the neglected or insignificant individuals of her own sex, who may happen to have been present. The other will have sought out the silent stranger—the poor relation—the plain woman—and all the most insignificant or unnoticed persons in the party. Especially she will have devoted herself to her own sex, and afforded to the company that rare, but noble illustration of female benevolence—a fascinating woman in company choosing to make herself agreeable to women.

If any action arising from vanity could be either commendable or great, I am disposed to think it would be so, for a woman to show that she could afford to tear herself away from the attentions of men, and devote her powers of pleasing to her own sex. The woman we have described, however, has feelings of a higher order. Her object is to use every gift she possesses for the happiness or the benefit of her fellow-creatures, and her benevolence prompts her to seek out those who are most in need of kindness and consideration. Forgetful of herself, she regards her ability to please as one of the talents committed to her trust, for the employment of which she must render an account at that awful tribunal where no selfish plea will be admitted. And thus she cultivates the art of conversation for the sake of increasing her usefulness, of consoling the distressed, of instructing the ignorant, and of beguiling of half their heaviness the necessary cares of life.

CHAPTER VII. DOMESTIC HABITS, —CONSIDERATION AND KINDNESS.

ON entering upon the subject of the domestic habits of the women of England, I feel the necessity of bearing in mind, that all individuals in the middle class of society, and even all who are connected with trade, are by no means under the same obligation to regard their own personal exertions as a duty. So far from this, there are unquestionably many in this class, who would be entirely out of their province, were they to engage in the manual occupations of their families and households. The possession of wealth has placed them, in these respects, on the same footing with the nobility, and they have, without doubt, an equal right to enjoy the luxuries which wealth can procure. I am, however, no less convinced that the absence of all necessity for personal exer- tion is a disadvantage to them, and that their happiness would be increased, if their situations in life were such as to present more imperative claims upon their individual services.

The virtue of considerateness refers strictly to the characters and circumstances of those around us. From the mistress of half a dozen servants, therefore, the same kind of consideration can never be required, as from the mistress of one; nor can the lady of a mansion, even though her husband should be engaged in trade, feel herself called to the same duties as the farmer's wife.

The considerateness I shall attempt to define is one of the highest recommendations the female character can possess; because it combines an habitual examination of our own situation and responsibilities, with a quick discernment of the character and feelings of those around us, and a benevolent desire to afford them as much pleasure, and spare them as much pain, as we can. A considerate woman, therefore, whether surrounded by all appliances and means of personal enjoyment, or depending upon the use of her own hands for the daily comforts of life, will look around her, and consider what is due to those whom Providence has placed within the sphere of her influence.

The man who voluntarily undertakes a difficult and responsible business, first inquires how it is to be conducted so as best to ensure success; so, the serious and thoughtful Woman, on entering upon the duties of domestic life, ascertains, by reflection and observation, in what manner they may be performed so as to render them most conducive to the great end she has in view—the promotion of the happiness of others; and as the man engaged in business does not run hither and thither, simply to make a show of alacrity, neither does the woman engaged in a higher and more important work, allow herself to be satisfied with her own willingness to do her duty, without a diligent and persevering investigation of what are the most effectual means by which it can be done.

Women are almost universally admonished of their duties in general terms, and hence they labour under great disadvantages. They are told to be virtuous; and in order to be so, they are advised to be kind and modest, orderly and discreet. But few teachers, and fewer writers, condescend to take up the minutiæ of everyday existence, so as to explain in what distinct and individual actions such kindness, modesty, order, and discretion consist. Indeed, the cases themselves, upon which these principles of right conduct are generally brought to bear, are so minute, and so apparently insignificant, that the writer who takes up this subject must not only be content to sacrifice all the dignity of authorship, but must submit occasionally to a smile of contempt for having filled a book with trifles.

In order, however, to ascertain the real importance of any point of merit, we should take into consideration its direct opposite. We never know the value of true kindness, so much as when contrasted with unkindness; and lest any one should think lightly of the virtue of consideration as a moral faculty, let us turn our attention to the character and habits of a woman who is without it. Such are not difficult to find, and we find them often in the lovely, and the seemingly amiable creatures of impulse, who rush about, with the impetus of the moment operating as their plea, uncontrollable affection their excuse, and sefishness, unknown to them, the moving spring at the bottom of their hearts. These individuals believe themselves to be so entirely governed by amiable feelings, that they not unfrequently boast of being kind—nay, too kind-hearted: but upon whom does their kindness tell, except upon themselves? It is true, they feel the impulse to be kind, and this impulse they gratify by allowing it to operate in any way that circumstances, or their own caprice, may point out. Yet, after all, how often is their kindness, for want of consideration, rendered wholly unavailable towards the promotion of any laudable or useful purpose.

Nor is this all. Want of consideration is often the occasion of absolute pain; and those, who because they deem it a recommendation to act from the impulse of the moment, will not take the trouble to reflect, are always, in a greater or less degree, liable to inflict misery upon others.

I remember walking home on a beautiful summer's evening, with one of these lovely and impetuous creatures, who was then just entering upon all the rights and privileges of a belle, and, to my great surprise, observing that she trod indiscriminately upon all the creeping things which the damp and the dew had tempted forth into our path. I remonstrated with her, of course; but she turned to me with her own bewitching air of naiveté, and said—"And pray, why may I not tread upon the snails? " Farther remonstrance was unnecessary, for the mind which had attained maturity without feeling enough to prevent this reckless and disgusting waste of life, must of necessity have been impervious to reason.

And thus it is with considerateness in general. If the season of youth glides over before habits of consideration are acquired, they will come tardily, and with little grace, in after life. Want of consideration for those of our fellow-creatures whose love is of importance to us, is not, however, a subject upon which we have so much cause for complaint. It is towards those with whom we are connected by social ties, without affection—and under this head, the situation of our servants and domestics claims the greatest care.

Servants are generally looked upon, by thoughtless young ladies, as a sort of household machinery; and when that machinery is of sufficient extent to operate upon every branch of the establishment, there can be no reason why it should not be brought into exercise, and kept in motion to any extent that may not be injurious. This machinery, however, is composed of individuals, possessing hearts as susceptible of certain kinds of feeling, as those of the more privileged beings, to whose comfort and convenience it is their daily business to minister. They know and feel that their lot in this world is comparatively hard; and if they are happily free from all presumptuous questionings of the wisdom and justice of Providence in placing them where they are, they are alive to the conviction that the burden of each day is sufficient, and often more than sufficient, for their strength.

In speaking of the obligation we are under to our domestics for their faithful services, it is no uncommon thing to be answered by this unmeaning remark; "They are well paid for what they do, " as if the bare fact of receiving food and clothing for their daily labour, placed them on the same footing with regard to comfort, as those who receive their food and clothing for doing nothing.

There is also another point of view in which this class of our fellow-creatures is very unfairly judged. Servants are required to have no faults. It is by no means uncommon to find the mistress of a family, who has enjoyed all the advantages of moral and even religious education, allowing herself to exhibit the most unqualified excess of indignation at the petty faults of a servant, who has never enjoyed either; and to hear her speak as if she was injured, imposed upon, insulted before her family, because the servant, who was engaged to work for her, had been betrayed into impertinence by a system of reproof as much at variance with christian meekness, as the retort it was so well calculated to provoke.

Women of such habits, would perhaps be a little surprised, if told, that when a lady descends from her own proper station, to speak in an irritating or injurious manner to a servant, she is herself guilty of impertinence, and that no domestic of honest and upright spirit will feel that such treatment ought to be submitted to.

On the other hand, there is a degree of kindness blended with dignity, which servants, who are not absolutely depraved, are able to appreciate; and the slight effort required to obtain their confidence, is almost invariably repaid by a double share of affectionate and faithful service.

The situation of living unloved by their domestics is one which I should hope there are few women capable of enduring with indifference. The cold attentions rendered without affection, and curtailed by every allowable means, the short unqualified reply to every question, the averted look, the privilege stolen rather than solicited, the secret murmur that is able to make itself understood without the use of words—all these are parts of a system of behaviour that chills the very soul, and forces upon the mind the unwelcome conviction, that a stranger who partakes not in our common lot, is within our domestic circle: or that an alien who enters not into the sphere of our home-associations, attends upon our social board; nay, so forcible is the impression, as almost to extend to a feeling, that an enemy is amongst the members of our own household.

How different is the impression produced by a manner calculated both to win their confidence and inspire their respect. The kind welcome after absence, the watchful eye, the anticipation of every wish, the thousand little attentions and acts of service beyond what are noted in the bond—who can resist the influence of these upon the heart, and not desire to pay them back—not certainly in their own kind and measure, but in the only way they can be returned consistently with the relative duties of both parties—in kindness and consideration?

It is not, however, in seasons of health and prosperity, that this bond between the different members of a family can be felt in its full force. There is no woman so happily circumstanced, but that she finds some link broken in the chain which binds her to this world—some shadow cast upon her earthly pictures. The best beloved are not always those who love the best; and expectation will exceed reality, even in the most favoured lot. There are hours of sadness that will steal in, even upon the sunny prime of life; and they are not felt the less, because it is sometimes impossible to communicate the reason for such sadness to those who are themselves the cause. In such cases, and while the heart is in some degree estranged from natural and familiar fellowship, we are thrown more especially upon the kindness and affection of our domestics, for the consolation we feel it impossible to live without. They may be, and they ought to be, wholly unacquainted with the cause of our disquietude; but a faithfully attached servant, without presuming beyond her proper sphere, is quick to discern the tearful eye, the gloomy brow, the countenance depressed; and it is at such times that their kindness, solicitude, and delicate attentions, might often put to shame the higher pretensions of superior refinement.

In cases of illness or death, it is perhaps more especially their merit to prove, by their indefatigable and unrequited assiduities, how much they make the interest of the family their own, and how great is their anxiety to remove all lighter causes of annoyance from interference with the great affliction in which those around them are involved. There is scarcely a more pitiable object in creation, than a helpless invalid left entirely to the care of domestics, whose affection never has been sought or won. But, on the other hand, the readiness with which they will sometimes sacrifice their needful rest, and that, night after night, to watch the feverish slumbers of a fretful invalid, is one of those redeeming features in the aspect of human nature, which it is impossible to regard without feelings of admiration and gratitude.

The question necessarily follows, —how are our domestics to be won over to this confidence and affection? It comes not by nature, for no tie, except what necessarily implies authority and subjection, exists between us. It cannot come by mutual acts of service, because the relation between us is of such a nature as to place the services almost entirely on their side, the benefits derived from such services, on ours. It comes, then, by instances of consideration, showing that we have their interests at heart in the same degree that we expect them to have ours. We cannot actually do much for them, because it would be out of our province, and a means of removing them out of theirs; but we can think and feel for them, and thus lighten or add weight to their burdens, by the manner in which our most trifling and familiar actions are performed.

In a foregoing CHAPTER, I have ventured a few hints on the subject of manners, chiefly as regards their influence amongst those who meet us upon equal terms in the social affairs of life. The influence of the manner we choose to adopt in our intercourse with servants, is of such importance as to deserve further notice than the nature of this work will allow.

There is a phenomenon sometimes witnessed at the head of a well-appointed table, from which many besides myself, have no doubt started with astonishment and disgust. A well-dressed, well-educated lady, attired in the most becoming and fashionable costume, is engaged in conversing with her friends, pressing them to partake of her well-flavoured viands, and looking and speaking with the blandest smiles; when suddenly one of the servants is beckoned towards her, and with an instantaneous expression of countenance, in which is concealed the passion and the imperiousness of a whole lifetime, he is admonished of his duty in sharp whispers that seem to hiss like lightning in his ears. The lady then turns round to her guests, is again arrayed in smiles, and prepared again to talk sweetly of the sympathies and amiabilities of our common nature.

There is, it must be confessed, a most objectionable manner, which blends familiarity with confidence; and this ought to be guarded against as much in reproof, as in commendation, for it cannot be expected that a mistress who reproves her servant with coarseness and vulgarity, will be treated with much delicacy in return. The consideration I would recommend, so far from inviting familiarity, is necessarily connected with true dignity, because it implies, in the most undeviating manner, a strict regard to the relative position of both parties. Let us see then in what it consists, or rather let us place it in a stronger light by pointing out instances in which the absence of it is most generally felt.

There are many young ladies, and some old ones, with whom the patronage of pets appears to be an essential part of happiness; and these pets, as various as the tastes they gratify, are all alike in one particular—they are all troublesome. If a lady engages her servants with an understanding that they are to wait upon her domestic animals, no one can accuse her of injustice. But if, with barely a sufficient number of domestics to perform the necessary labour of her household, she establishes a menagerie, and expects the hard-working servants to undertake the additional duty of waiting upon her pets—perhaps the most repulsive creatures in existence, to them—such additional service ought at least to be solicited as a favour; and she will have no right to feel indignant, should the favour be sometimes granted in a manner neither gracious nor conciliating.

When a servant who has been all day labouring hard to give an aspect of comfort and cleanliness to the particular department committed to her care, sees the young ladies of the family come home from their daily walk, and, never dreaming of her, or her hard labour, trample over the hall and stairs without stopping to rid themselves of that incumbrance of clay, which a fanciful writer has classed amongst the "miseries of human life; " is it to be expected that the servant who sees this, should be so far uninfluenced by the passions of humanity, as not to feel the stirrings of rage and resentment in her bosom? And when this particular act is repeated every day, and followed up by others of the same description, the frequently recurring sensations of rage and resentment, so naturally excited, will strengthen into those of habitual dislike, and produce that cold service, and grudging kindness, which have already been described.

There are thousands of little acts of this description, such as ordering the tired servants to rise at an unseasonable hour to prepare an early breakfast, and then not being ready yourself before the usual time—

being habitually too late for dinner, without any sufficient reason, and having a second dinner served up—ringing the bell for the servant to leave her washing, cooking, or cleaning, and come up to you, to receive orders to fetch your thimble or scissors from the highest apartment in the house—all which need no comment; and surely those servants must be more than human, who can experience the effects of such a system of behaviour, carried on for days, months, and years, and not feel, and feel bitterly, that they are themselves regarded as mere machines, while their comfort and convenience is as much left out of calculation, as if they were nothing more.

It is an easy thing, on entering a family, to ascertain whether the female members of it are, or are not considerate. Where they are not, there exists, as a necessary consequence, a constant series of murmurings, pleadings, remonstrances, and attempted justifications, which sadly mar the happiness of the household. On the other hand, where the female members of a family are considerate, there is a secret spring of sympathy linking all hearts together, as if they were moved by a simultaneous impulse of kindness on one side, and gratitude on the other. Few words have need to be spoken, few professions to be made, for each is hourly discovering that they have been the subject of affectionate solicitude, and they are consequently on the watch for every opportunity of making an adequate return. If the brother comes home sad or weary, the sister to whom he has pledged himself to some exertion, detects the languor of his eye, and refrains from pressing upon him a fulfilment of his promise; if the sister is labouring under depression, the brother feels himself especially called upon to stand forward as her friend; and if one of the family be suffering even slightly from indisposition, there are watchful eyes around, and the excursion is cheerfully given up by one, the party by another, and a quiet social evening is unanimously agreed upon to be spent at home, and agreed upon in such a way as that the invalid shall never suspect it has been done at the cost of any pleasure.

There is no proof of affection more kindly prompted and more gratefully received, than that of easily detecting uncomplained-of indisposition. We might almost single out this faculty as the surest test of love—for who observes the incipient wrinkle on a stranger's brow, or marks the gradually-increasing paleness of an unloved cheek? Or what can convince us more effectually that we are in a world of strangers, to whom our interests are as nothing, than to be pressed on every hand to do, what our bodily strength is unequal to.

There are points of consideration in which we often practise great self-deception. "Don't you think it would do you good, my dear? " asks the young lady of her sickly sister, when the day of promised pleasure is at hand, and she begins to fear her sister's cough will render it impossible to go from home. "The pain in your foot, my love, is considerably better, " says the wife to her husband, when she thinks the fashionables are about leaving Bath. "You are looking extremely well, " says the niece to her aged uncle, who has promised to take her to Paris; "I think I never saw you look so well. " But all this is not love. It does not feel like love to the parties addressed; for nature is true to herself, and she will betray the secrets of art. How different are the workings of that deep and earnest affection that sees with one glance how unreasonable it would be to drag forth the invalid to any participation in the enjoyments of health; and how welcome is the gentle whisper which assures us that one watchful eye perceives our suffering, one sympathizing ear participates in our weakness and distress: for it is distress to be compelled to complain that we are unequal to do, what the happiness of others depends upon our doing; and never is the voice of friendship employed in a more kindly office, than when pleading the cause of our infirmity.

It is chiefly with regard to the two sister virtues of consideration and kindness, that I look upon the women of England as so highly privileged; because the nature of their social and domestic circumstances is such, as to afford them constantly-recurring opportunities of proving that they think often and kindly of others, without any departure from the wonted routine of their conduct, that might wear the character of a pointed application of such feelings.

It has a startling, and by no means agreeable effect upon the mind, when a woman who is not habitually accustomed to any sort of practical kindness, so far deviates from her usual line of conduct, as to perform any personal service solely for ourselves. We feel that she has been troubled, and suspect that she has been annoyed. But women accustomed to practical duties are able to turn the whole tide of their affectionate solicitude into channels so wholesome and salutary, that our pride is not wounded by the obligation under which we are placed, nor is our sense of gratitude impaired by the pain of being singled out as the object of unwonted and elaborate attentions.

In order to illustrate the subject by a familiar instance, let us imagine one of those events experienced by all who lived to years of maturity, and experienced in such a way as to have thrown them in a peculiar manner, upon the domestic comforts of the circle to which they were introduced—the arrival, after long travel, on a visit to an early and highly-valued friend.

It is not necessary to this picture, that park gates should be thrown open, and footmen stationed on the steps of the hall; it will better serve our purpose, that the mistress of the house should herself be the first to meet her guest, with that genuine welcome in her looks and manner, that leaves nothing to be expressed by words. We will suppose that with her own hand she displaces all the encumbrance of extra wrappings, rendered necessary by the winter's journey, and having quietly dismissed the expectant chaise-driver or porter, she leads her friend into the neatly furnished parlour, where another and a more familiar welcome seems at once to throw open her heart and her house for her reception. A fire that has been designedly built up, is then most energetically stirred, until a bright and genial blaze diffuses its light round the room, and the guest begins to glow with the two-fold warmth of a welcome and a winter's fire.

In the mean time, the servant, well taught in the mysteries of hospitality, conveys the luggage upstairs unseen, and the guest is led to the chamber appointed for her nightly rest. There most especially, is both seen and felt, the kind feeling that has taken into account her peculiar tastes, and anticipated all her well-remembered wishes. The east or the west apartment has been chosen, according to the preference she has been known to express in days long since gone by, when she and her friend were girls together; and thus the chain of fond and cherished recollections is made to appear again unbroken after the lapse of years, and a conviction is silently impressed upon the mind of the traveller—perhaps the most welcome of all earthly sources of assurance—that we have been remembered, not merely in the abstract—but that through long, long years of change and separation, time has not obliterated from the mind of a dear friend, the slightest trace of our individuality.

Perhaps none can tell until they have arrived at middle age, what is in reality the essential sweetness of this conviction. In our association with the world, we may have obtained for our industry, our usefulness, or it may be for our talents, a measure of approval, at least commensurate with our deserts; but give back to the worn and the weary in this world's warfare, the friends of their early youth—the friends who loved them, faults and all—the friends who could note down their very follies without contempt, and who attached a degree of interest and importance to the trifling peculiarities of their temper and feelings, which rendered them indelible memorials of an attachment such as never can be formed in after life.

To return from this digression—The English woman, in the unsophisticated beauty of her character, has a power far surpassing what can be attained by the most scrupulous observance of the rules of art, of thus investing her familiar and social actions with a charm that goes directly to the heart.

We have traced the traveller to the chamber of her rest, and it is not in the choice of this room alone, but in its furniture and general aspect, that she reads the cheering truth of a superintending care having been exercised over all it contains, in strict reference to herself, not merely as an honoured guest, but as a lover of this or that small article of comfort or convenience, which in the world of comparative strangers amongst whom she has been living, she has seldom thought it worth her while to stipulate for, and still less frequently has had referred to her choice.

Now, it is evident that the mistress of the house herself must have been here. With her own hand she must have placed upon the table the favourite toilet-cushion, worked by a friend who was alike dear to herself and her guest. With her own hand she must have selected the snow-white linen, and laid out, not in conspicuous obtrusiveness, a few volumes calculated for the hours of silent meditation, when her friend shall be alone.

It is impossible that the services of the most faithful domestic should be able to convey half the heartfelt meaning indicated by these few familiar acts, so richly worth their cost. It is not from the circumstance of having all our wants supplied, that the most lively satisfaction is derived; it is from the cheering fact that we ourselves, in our individual capacity, have been the object of so much faithful recollection, and untiring love.

Instead therefore of regarding it as a subject for murmuring and complaint, that her means of personal indulgence do not supply her with a greater number of domestics, the true English woman ought rather to esteem it a privilege that her station in life is such, as to place her in the way of imparting this rational and refined enjoyment.

We cannot imagine the first day of hospitable welcome complete without our visiter being introduced to that concatenation of comforts—an early tea. On descending from her chamber, then, she finds all things in readiness for this grateful and refreshing meal. Her attention is not distracted by apologies for what is not there—but what, on such occasions, frequently might have been, at the cost of half the effort required for an elaborate excuse. As if the fairy order had been at work, the table is spread with all things most agreeable after weary travel; and the guest, instead of being pressed to eat with such assiduity that she begins to think her visit has no other object, is only interrupted by kind inquiries relating to home associations, and is beguiled into a prolongation of her meal, by being drawn out into a detail of the events of her journey.

As the evening passes on, their conversation becomes more intimate, and while it deepens in interest, that full expansion of the soul takes place, under which, whatever English women may be in the superficial intercourse of polished life, I have no scruple in saying, that as fireside companions, they are the most delightful upon earth. There are such vivid imaginings, such touches of native humour, such deep well-springs of feeling, beyond their placid exterior, that when they dare to come forth, and throw themselves upon the charity or affection of their hearers, one is beguiled into a fascination the more intense, because it combines originality of thought with gentle manners, and in a peculiar and forcible way invests the cherished recollections of the past, with the fresh warm colouring of the present hour.

It is not amidst congregated masses of society, that the true English woman can exhibit her native powers of conversation. It is when two are met together, with perhaps a husband or a brother for a third, and the midnight hour steals on, and yet they take no note of time, for they are opening out their separate store of treasures from the deep of memory, sharing them with each other, and blending all with such bright anticipations of the future, as none but a woman's imagination can enjoy, with faith in their reality.

Or, perhaps, they are consulting upon some difficult point of duty, or sympathizing with each other in affliction; and then, where shall we look but to the English woman for the patient listener, the faithful counsellor, the staunch supporter of each virtuous purpose, the keen discerner in points of doubtful merit, and the untiring comforter in every hour of need.

It would be too tedious, and might to some appear too trifling, were I to trace out the conduct of the being here described, through more of the familiar scenes presented by domestic life. It may also be thought by some who know little of women in this capacity, that I am drawing merely from imagination: others will know that my colouring is true—that human life, in some of its obscurest passages, has secrets of moral excellence in the female character, presenting objects as lovely as ever were revealed to the poet's fancy. Alas! for those whose memory alone supplies them with the materials for this picture—who now can only feel that "such things were! "

The charge of trifling is one I should be sorry to incur in writing on a subject so serious as the domestic morals of women; yet how to enter into a detail sufficiently minute without, I confess I do not clearly see. I must, therefore, again pause, and ask the reader, in my own defence, of what the ordinary life of a woman of the middle class of society is composed but a mass of trifles, out of which arises the happiness or the misery of a numerous and important portion of the human race? I would also ask, What is a woman who despises trifles? She may possibly enjoy, with undisputed dignity, a niche in the temple of fame, but she ought never to descend from her marble pedestal, to mingle with the social circle around the living blaze of the domestic hearth. Those quiet, unobtrusive virtues, which are ever the most lovely in the female character, must necessarily be the most difficult to define. They are so much more felt than seen—so much better understood than described—that to give them a name would be impossible, and even to portray them in an ideal picture might not perhaps convey to the mind of the beholder, any adequate idea of their importance. But, as in painting a finished picture, the skill of the artist is not only required in the general outline, but is equally requisite in the filling-up, so the perfection of the female character, is not sufficiently indicated by saying she is possessed of every virtue, unless we point out the individual instances upon which those virtues are brought to bear; and the more minute and delicate their aspect, if they are but frequently presented to our notice, the stronger is our conviction that virtuous principle is the ground-work of the whole.

With regard to the particular instance already described, the case may perhaps be more clearly illustrated by adding a picture of an opposite description, in order to ascertain in what particular points the two cases differ.

For this purpose, we will imagine a woman distinguished by no extreme of character, receiving her guest under precisely the same circumstances as the one already described. In this case, the visiter is permitted to see that her hostess has reluctantly laid down her book at the latest possible period of time which politeness would allow; or, after her guest has remained twenty minutes in a vacant, and by no means inviting parlour, she comes toiling up from the kitchen, with a countenance that makes it dreadful to be adding to her daily fatigues by placing one's self at her table; and she answers the usual inquiries of her friend, as to her state of health, with a minute detail of the various phenomena of a headach with which she has that morning been attacked. The one domestic is then called up—and wo betide that family, whose daily services, unpractised by its individual members towards each other, all emanate from one domestic.

When one domestic then is ordered, in the hearing of the guest, to take all the luggage up stairs, to bring hot water, towels, soap—to turn the carpets—run for the best looking-glass—and see that tea is ready by the time the friend comes down. The party then ascend, accompanied by the panting servant, into a room, upon which no kind care has been bestowed. It may possibly be neat—so neat that the guest supposes it never has been, and is not yet intended to be, used. Yes, every thing is in its place; but a general blank pervades the whole, and it is not the least of the disappointments experienced by our guest, that she finds no water to refresh her aching temples. The mistress of the house is angry at this neglect, and rings the bell. The servant ascends from the kitchen to the highest room, to learn that she must go down again, and return, before half the catalogue of her faults has been told.

On such errands as this, she is employed until the party descend to the parlour, where the bell is again rung more imperatively, and tea is ordered to be brought instanter. In the mean time, the fire has dwindled to the lowest bar. The mistress looks for coals, but the usual receptacle is empty. She feels as if there were a conspiracy against her. There is—there can be no one to blame but the servant; and thus her chagrin is alleviated by complaints against servants in general, and her own in particular. With these complaints, and often-repeated apologies, the time is occupied until the appearance of the long-expected meal, when the guest is pressed to partake of a repast not sweetened by the comments of her hostess, or the harassed and forlorn appearance of an overworked domestic.

The mistress of this house may all the while be glad to see her guest, and may really regard her as an intimate and valued friend; but never having made it an object to practise the domestic virtue of making others happy, she knows not how to convey any better idea of a welcome than by words. She therefore sets deliberately to work to describe how happy she esteems herself in receiving so dear a friend—wishes some third party were at home—hopes to be able to amuse her—tells of the parties she has engaged for each successive evening—brings out a pile of engravings—fears her guest is weary—and lastly, at a very early hour, rings for the chamber-candlesticks presuming that her visitor would like to retire.

It is needless to observe that the generality of visiters do retire upon this hint; and it is equally needless to add, that the individual here described fails to exhibit the character of the true English woman, whose peculiar charm is that of diffusing happiness, without appearing conspicuously as the agent in its diffusion. It is from the unseen, but active principle of disinterested love, ever working at her heart, that she enters, with a perception as delicate as might be supposed to belong to a ministering angel, into the peculiar feelings and tones of character influencing those around her, applying the magical key of sympathy to all they suffer or enjoy, to all they fear or hope, until she becomes identified as it were with their very being, blends her own existence with theirs, and makes her society essential to their highest earthly enjoyment.

If a heightened degree of earthly enjoyment were all we could expect to obtain by this line of conduct, I should still be disposed to think the effect produced would be richly worth our pains. But I must again repeat, that the great aim of a christian woman will always be, so to make others happy, that their feelings shall be attuned to the reception of better thoughts than those which relate to mere personal enjoyment—so to make others happy, as to win them over to a full perception of the loveliness of those christian virtues which her own life and conduct consistently show forth.

CHAPTER VIII. DOMESTIC HABITS—CONSIDERATION AND KINDNESS.

THE subject of consideration might be continued to almost any extent, since it seems either to comprehend, or to be closely connected with, all that is morally excellent in woman. We shall, however, confine our attention to only a few more of those important branches in which this fertile theme demands our serious thought—towards those who are beneath us in pecuniary circumstances, and towards those with whom we are associated in the nearest domestic relations.

The young and inexperienced having never themselves tasted the cup of adversity, are, in a great measure, excusable for not knowing how to treat the morbid and susceptible feelings, which the fact of having drank deeply of that cup often produces; nor is it easy to communicate to their minds any idea of the extreme of suffering to which this tone of feeling may extend. Much may be done, however, by cultivating habits of consideration, by endeavouring sometimes to identify themselves with those who suffer, by asking how it would be with them if their parents had fallen below what, by the world, is called respectability—if they were obliged to seek the means of maintaining themselves—if they were admitted into families by sufferance, and only on condition that they should remain until another home could be found, in which their own hands might minister to their necessities.

There is no class of beings whose circumstances altogether are more calculated to call forth our tenderest sympathies, than those delicate females whose fireside comforts are broken up by the adverse turn of their pecuniary affairs, and who are consequently sent forth to share the lot of families unknown to them, and to throw themselves upon the kindness and consideration of strangers. It is in cases of this kind, especially, that we see the importance of having cultivated the moral faculties, of having instilled into the mind those sound principles of integrity, usefulness, and moral responsibility, which, in proportion as they become the foundation of our familiar and daily conduct, necessarily invest every act of duty with a cheerfulness which cannot fail to be acceptable in the sight of that merciful Creator, who alone is capable of transforming what is irksome or repulsive to the natural feelings, into sources of gratitude and delight.

The frequent occurrence of such changes in the pecuniary affairs of English families, as render it necessary for the female members to be thus circumstanced, is, therefore, one amongst the many reasons, why the effects of that false refinement which is gradually increasing amongst the female part of English society, should be counteracted by the strenuous efforts of the well-wishers of their country; and high time it is, that all our energies should be roused, not by any means to retard the progress of intellect, but to force along with it the growth of sound principles, and the increase of moral power.

Persons who are reduced in their pecuniary circumstances are generally judged of as we judge our servants, and those who are born to humble means; they are required to have no faults, and the public cry is especially directed against them, if they evince the least symptom of pride. Indeed, so great is our abhorrence of this particular fault, that we often make even a slight evidence of its existence a plea for the discontinuance of our bounty and our favour. We forget that the pride of the individuals in question has perhaps been ministered to throughout the whole of their former lives, and that they, no more than we, can renounce their soul-besetting sins, as they give up the luxuries they are no longer able to procure. We forget, also, that their circumstances are calculated, in an especial manner, to rouse the lurking evil, even had it never been conspicuous in their characters before.

The man who floats safely upon the stream of worldly prosperity, with his early companions a little lower than himself, can afford to be gracious and conciliating; but when he begins to sink, and feels the same companions struggling to float past him, and finally leaving him to contend with his difficulties, his feelings towards them undergo a total change: he accounts himself an injured man, and becomes a prey to envy, disappointment, and wounded pride. The world's contumely, more grievous than his actual privations, assails his peace of mind; he learns to look for unkindness, and to expect it even where it does not exist. In the stranger's eye he reads contempt and neglect; he lives, as it were, surrounded by daggers— bleeding at every pore, and wounded by every thing with which he comes in contact. "How absurd! " is the exclamation we hear from the prosperous and inconsiderate—"how worse than absurd for a man to be feeling in this manner, because he has lost a few hundreds! " And yet men do feel to such a degree, that nothing but religion can enable them to bear such vicissitudes with calmness and resignation. And even when supported by religion, it has pleased our heavenly Father to accompany these dispensations of his providence, with a degree of suffering to which no human mind is insensible.

It is generally regarded as the extreme of benevolence, if, in our intercourse with such persons, we treat them exactly as we did in more prosperous days; and few there are who can at all times withhold expressions equivalent to these: "How unreasonable it is to expect so much attention now! It is not likely we can ask that family to meet our friends; we should be willing still to notice them in a private way, if they would but be more grateful—more considerate. " And thus they are allowed to pass away from our social gatherings, to be called upon perhaps occasionally at their own humble abodes, but by no means to be invited in return, lest some of our wealthier friends should detect us in the act of performing the offices of hospitality to a person in a threadbare coat. And yet this family may have done nothing worse than thousands are doing every day—than even our richest and dearest friends are doing— and we may know it all the while.

It sickens the heart to think of these things, and to reflect how far— how very far, even the good and the kind fall short of that beautiful and heart-touching injunction of our blessed Saviour, "When thou makest a feast, call the poor, the maimed, the lame, the blind. "

The wealthy and distinguished man, with whom we have but a slight acquaintance, sends his son into our neighbourhood on business or pleasure. We hear of his coming, and persuade ourselves it is but respectful to invite him to be our guest. It is at the expense of our domestic comfort that we entertain him—but that is nothing. Difficulties appear on every hand, to vanish as soon as they appear; we even persuade ourselves that a sort of merit attaches to our doing all in our power to accommodate the son of so distinguished a person.

The poor widow, perhaps our relative, sends her son to town to seek a situation, and we hear of his coming. We knew his mother in more prosperous days. She was a worthy woman then, but her husband died insolvent, and the family necessarily fell away from what they had been. It cannot be at all incumbent upon us to ask such young men as these to our houses. They might come in shoals. Our domestic comfort would be sacrificed, and it is the duty of every one to maintain the peace and order of their own household.

Thus the widow's son is allowed to wander up and down the streets, to resort to expensive lodging-houses, and to purchase, with the pittance provided by his mother from her slender means, that accommodation which a little christian hospitality might have spared him.

We complain that our streets are thronged on the Sabbath-day with troops of idle young men and women, who afford a painful spectacle to those who pass them on their way to public worship. How many of these—apprentices, and assistants in business—are actually driven into the streets from very want of any thing like a hospitable or social home!

I am by no means prepared to say, how far true christian benevolence, acted out towards this class of the community, would lead us to give up our domestic comfort for their sakes, and for the sake of preserving them from harm; but I do know it would lead us to adopt a very different treatment of them, from that which generally prevails; and I consider also, that these duties rest especially with women.

It is not easy for a man who has to fill the office of master to a number of apprentices and assistants during the hours of business, to unbend before them at his own fireside. But a considerate and high-principled woman, may, without loss of dignity, and certainly without loss of respect, make them feel that she regards it as her duty to be their friend as well as their mistress, and that she looks upon herself as under a sacred obligation to advise them in difficulties, to guard their welfare, and to promote their comfort, simply because the all-wise Disposer of human affairs has seen meet to place them within the sphere of her influence.

I have devoted a CHAPTER to the influence of English women. Many CHAPTERs might be filled with the duties of tradesmen's wives towards the young people employed in their husband's affairs, and the responsibility attaching to them, for the tone of moral character which such persons exhibit through the whole of their after lives. Of how little value, in this point of view, is the immense variety of accomplishments generally acquired at school, compared with the discrimination and tact that would enable a woman to extend her influence among the class of persons here described, and the principle that would lead her to turn such influence to the best account. How many a mother's heart would be made glad by finding, when her son returned to his home, that he had experienced something of a mother's kindness from his master's wife; and how many a father would rejoice that his child had been preserved from the temptations of a city life, by the good feeling that was cherished and kept alive at his master's fireside!

It is for circumstances such as these, that a large proportion of the young women of England, now undergoing the process of education, have to prepare. Not to imitate the heroines they read of; but to plunge into the actual cares, and duties, and responsibilities of every-day existence. They will probably have little time either for drawing or music, may seldom be spoken to in a foreign tongue, and hardly have an opportunity of displaying half the amount of verbal knowledge with which their memories have been stored. But they will, if they are at all intent upon fulfilling the great end of their existence, have to bethink themselves every hour, what is best to be done for the good and the happiness of those around them. For this great and laudable purpose, it is of the highest importance that they should cultivate habits of consideration, for how else can they expect to enter into the states of mind, and modes of feeling of those with whom they associate, so as to render the means they use effectual to the end desired?

It happens to almost all families, in the middle rank of life in England, that they are directly or remotely connected with relatives whose pecuniary means are much more limited than their own. To these, as well as to persons of recently decayed fortune, it is generally thought highly meritorious to extend the common courtesies of society. It implies no disrespect to this class of individuals, to call them poor relations; since the poor are often brought into a state of wholesome discipline, which eventually places them higher than the rich in the scale of moral worth. The poor relation may possibly have known in very early life what it was to enjoy all the comforts that ample means afford; but she becomes at last a sort of useful appendage to an uncle's or a brother's family, or is invited by her cousins whenever they happen to be in arrears with their plain-work—when one of the family wants nursing through a tedious illness—or when they are going abroad, and require some one to overlook the household in their absence.

The poor relation, in the first place, is shown upstairs into a kind of tolerable attic, where the walls are whitewashed, and where a little bed with blue-check curtains is prepared for her accommodation.

They hope she will not mind sleeping in the attic—indeed they are sure she will not, she is such a dear, good creature; besides, they all like the attic for the view it commands, and mamma says it is the most comfortable room in the house: yet, somehow or other, the young ladies never sleep in the attic themselves; and considering it is the most desirable room in the house, and commands so excellent a view, it is astonishingly seldom occupied.

The poor relation is then introduced to company without a name—is spoken of as the person staying at Mrs. So and So's; and, after being told that she need not sit longer than is agreeable to her after meals, is fairly installed into office, by being informed, that the south chamber is very warm without a fire, and has a good light too, so that she can see an hour longer there than in any other. Here the different members of the family bring their work for her to do, looking round every time they enter, with a hope that she does not feel cold. From the young lady of twenty years, to the child of three, a demand is made upon her for the supply of all absent buttons, and all broken strings. All the stockings hoarded up against her coming are brought to her to be darned—all borders to quill—all linen to be mended: and this inundation of work is the natural consequence of her having shown symptoms of a desire to be generally agreeable; but if no such desire has been exhibited, wo betide the poor relation who proposes a visit to a rich one, where kindly feeling and habits of consideration have never been cultivated.

I remember it was very startling to me in my youth, and appeared to me at that time a contradiction in human nature, that, while people had comfortable homes, and were surrounded by everything that could minister to enjoyment, they were often invited out to partake of the enjoyments of their friends, and so pressed to prolong such visits, that it seemed as if their friends could never be weary of their society. But, let the same individuals have no home, let them be placed in circumstances calculated to render an invitation peculiarly acceptable, and it was with difficulty obtained, or not obtained at all. Though in all respects as agreeable as in former days, they were not pressed to stay beyond a very limited period; and some who had been the most solicitous to enjoy the favour of their company, suddenly found their accommodations so exceedingly small, that they could not invite any guest to partake of their hospitality.

But these, my sisters, are disgraceful ways, for woman—warm-hearted, generous, noble-minded woman, to fall into. From men we expect not all those little niceties of behaviour and feeling that would tend to heal the wounds of adversity. Their necessary pursuits deprive them of many opportunities of making the unfortunate and afflicted feel, that, amidst the wreck of their worldly hopes, they have at least retained some moral dignity in the estimation of their friends; but from woman we do look for some redeeming charities, some tenderness of heart among the sordid avocations and selfish pursuits of this life; and never do they rise to such true eminence, as when they bestow these charities, and apply this tenderness to the broken in spirit, the neglected, and the desolate, who are incapable of rendering them any return.

Harassed by the cares and perplexities of a sordid world, and disappointed in the high promise of our early youth; neglected, perhaps despised, where we had hoped to find protection and support in the hour of trial; driven out from the temples of our soul's idolatry; it is to woman that we look for the mantle of charity, to cast over the blighted bosom—for the drop of sweetness, to mingle with our bitter cup. We stretch our eyes over the wide tumultuous ocean of life, for some spot on which our ark may rest. We send forth the raven, and it returns not; but the gentler dove comes back with the olive-branch, and we hail it as a harbinger of safety and peace.

Although it must be confessed that women are sometimes too negligent of the tender offices of kindness towards those who have no immediate claim upon their affections, there remains some excuse for this particular species of culpability, in the general usages of society, and in the example of discreet and prudent persons, who deem it unsafe to deviate in any conspicuous manner from the beaten track of custom. No excuse, however, can be found for those who permit the closer ties of relationship to exist, without endeavouring to weave into the same bond all the tender sympathies of which the human heart is capable.

Brothers and sisters are so associated in English homes, as materially to promote each other's happiness, by the habits of kindness and consideration which they cultivate; and when a strong friendship can be formed between such parties, it is perhaps one of the most faithful and disinterested of any which the aspect of human life presents. A young man of kind and social feelings is often glad to find in his sister, a substitute for what he afterwards ensures more permanently in a wife; and young women are not backward in returning this affection by a love as confiding, and almost as tender as they are capable of feeling. Their intercourse has also the endearing charm of early association, which no later-formed acquaintance can supply. They have shared the sunny hours of childhood together; and when the young man goes forth into the world, the love of his sister is like a talisman about his heart. Women, however, must be watchful and studious to establish this intimate connexion, and to keep entire the golden cord by which they are thus bound. Affection does not come by relationship alone; and never yet was the affection of man fully and lastingly engaged by woman, without some means being adopted on her part to increase or preserve his happiness. The childish and most unsatisfactory fondness that means nothing but "I love you, " goes but a little way to reach the heart of man; but let his home be made more comfort- able, let his peculiarities of habit and temper be studiously consulted, and social and familiar gratifications provided for his daily use; and, unless he is ungrateful beyond the common average of mankind, he will be sure to regard the source from whence his comforts flow with extreme complacency, and not unfrequently with affection.

On the other hand, let the sister possess all that ardour of attachment which young ladies are apt to believe they feel, let her hang about his neck at parting, and bathe his face with her tears; if she has not taken the trouble to rise and prepare his early meal, but has allowed him to depend upon the servant, or to prepare it for himself; it is very questionable whether that brother can be made to believe in her affection; and certainly he will be far from feeling its value. If, again, they read some interesting volume together, if she lends her willing sympathy, and blends her feelings with his, entering into all the trains of thought and recollection which two congenial minds are capable of awakening in each other; and if, after the book is closed, he goes up into his chamber late on the Saturday night, and finds his linen unaired, buttonless, and unattended to, with the gloves he had ten times asked to have mended, remaining untouched, where he had left them; he soon loses the impression of the social hour he had been spending, and wishes, that, instead of an idle sister, he had a faithful and industrious wife. He reasons, and reasons rightly, that while his sister is willing to share with him all that is most agreeable to herself, she is by no means willing to do for his sake what is not agreeable, and he concludes his argument with the conviction, that notwithstanding her professions, hers is not true affection.

I do not mean that sisters ought to be the servants of their brothers, or that they should not, where domestics abound, leave the practical part of these duties to them. All that is wanted is stronger evidence of their watchfulness and their solicitude for their brother's real comfort. The manner in which this evidence shall be given, must still be left to their judgment, and their circumstances. There are, however a few simple rules, by which I should suppose all kindly affectioned women would be willing to be guided. No woman in the enjoyment of health should allow her brother to prepare his own meals at any time of the day, if it were possible for her to do it for him. No woman should allow her brother to put on linen in a state of dilapidation, to wear gloves or stockings in want of mending, or to return home without finding a neat parlour, a place to sit down without asking for it, and a cheerful invitation to partake of necessary refreshment.

All this I believe is often faithfully done, where the brother is a gentlemanly, attractive, and prepossessing person—in short, a person to be proud of in company, and pleased with in private; but a brother is a brother still, even where these attractions do not exist: where the duty is most irksome, the moral responsibility is precisely the same, as where it is most pleasing. Besides, who knows what female influence may not effect? It is scarcely probable that a younger brother, treated by his sisters with perpetual contempt, almost bordering upon disgust, regarded as an intolerable bore, and got rid of by every practicable means, will grow up into a companionable, interesting, and social man; or if he should, he would certainly reserve these qualities for exercise beyond the circle of his own fireside, and for the benefit of those who could appreciate him better than his sisters.

The virtue of consideration, in the intercourse of sisters with brothers, is never more felt than in the sacred duty of warning them of moral evil, and encouraging them in moral good. Here we see in an especial manner the advantages arising from habits of personal attention and kindness. A woman who stands aloof from the common offices of domestic usefulness, may very properly extend her advice to a husband, a brother, or a son; but when she has faithfully pointed out the fault she would correct, she must leave the object of her solicitude, with his wounded self-love unhealed, and his irritated feelings unrelieved. She has done her duty, and the impression most frequently remaining upon the mind of the other party is, either that she has done it in anger, or that it is impossible she can love a being of whom she entertains such hard thoughts.

The sister who is accustomed to employ her hands in the services of domestic life, is, on these occasions, rich in resources. She feels the pain she has been compelled to give, and calculates how much she has to make up. It is a time for tenfold effort; but it must be effort without display. In a gentle and unobtrusive manner, she does some extra service for her brother, choosing what would otherwise be degrading in its own nature, in order to prove in the most delicate manner, that though she can see a fault in him, she still esteems herself his inferior, and though she is cruel enough to point it out, her love is yet so deep and pure as to sweeten every service she can render him.

It is impossible for the human heart to resist this kind of evidence, and hence arises the strong influence that women possess over the moral feelings of those with whom they are intimately associated.

If such, then, be the effect of kindness and consideration upon the heart of man, what must we expect when it operates in all its force and all its sweetness upon that of woman. In her intercourse with man, it is impossible but that woman should feel her own inferiority; and it is right that it should be so. Yet, feeling this, it is also impossible but that the weight of social and moral duties she is called upon to perform, must, to an unsanctified spirit, at times appear oppressive. She has innumerable sources of disquietude, too, in which no man can partake; and from the very weakness and susceptibility of her own nature, she has need of sympathies which it would be impossible for him to render. She does not meet him upon equal terms. Her part is to make sacrifices, in order that his enjoyment may be enhanced. She does this with a willing spirit; but, from error of judgment, or from want of consideration, she does it so often without producing any adequate result, and so often without grateful acknowledgment, that her spirit sometimes sinks within her, and she shrinks back from the cares and anxieties of every day, with a feeling that the burden of life is too heavy to be borne.

Nor is man to be blamed for this. He knows not half the foolish fears that agitate her breast. He could not be made to know, still less to understand, the intensity of her capability of suffering, from slight, and what to him would appear inadequate causes. But women do know what their sex is formed to suffer; and for this very reason, there is sometimes a bond existing between sisters, the most endearing, the most pure and disinterested, of any description of affection which this world affords.

I am the more inclined to think that the strength of this bond arises chiefly out of their mutual knowledge of each other's capability of receiving pain; because, in families whose circumstances are uniformly easy, and who have never known the visitation of any deep affliction, we often see the painful spectacle of sisters forming obstacles to each other in their progress, both to temporal and eternal happiness. They seem to think the hey-day of life so unlikely to be clouded, that they can afford, wantonly and perversely, to intercept the sunshine that would otherwise fall upon each other's path; or to calculate so confidently upon the continued smooth- ness of the stream of time, that they sportively drive each other upon the rocks and the quicksands, which, even in the glad season of youth, will occasionally appear; while the very fact of knowing each other's weak points of character, while it ought to excite their utmost tenderness, only affords them subjects for tormenting sarcasm and biting scorn.

I have heard of hackney-coachmen in a certain highly-civilized metropolis, who adopt the cruel practice of lashing a galled or wounded part, if they can find one in the wretched animals they drive; but I hardly think the practice, abhorrent as it is, demands our condemnation more than that of the women who are thus false and cruel to each other—who, because they know exactly where to wound, apply the instrument of torture to the mind, unsparingly, and with the worst effect.

Let us glance hastily over the humiliating supposition that such a propensity does actually exist amongst women. Let us glance hastily, too, over the long train of minute and irremediable evils which the exercise of such a propensity is calculated to produce—the wounded feeling, the imagined injury, the suspicious dread, the bitter retort, and the secretly-cherished revenge. It is not enough for those who practise such habits to say, "I mean no harm: I love my sister, and would do her any signal service in my power. " Opportunities of performing signal services do not often fall in our way; but while we wait for these, we have opportunities innumerable of soothing or irritating the feelings of others, as our own dispositions prompt—of repelling or attracting—of weaning affection, or of inspiring confidence; —and these ends are easily obtained, by the manner in which we conduct ourselves towards those whom Providence has placed immediately around us.

So many young women, however, escape the censure here implied, by their self-complacency on the score of general kindness, that it may, perhaps, be as well to speak more explicitly on this important subject. It is not, then, to direct unkindness that I refer, but to that general absence of kind consideration, which produces the same effect. Perhaps one sister is unreasonably elated at the success of some of her plans: and in the midst of her extatic joy she finds herself mimicked with all the air of ineffable contempt, by another. Perhaps one sister is rather unusually depressed in spirits from some incommunicable cause: the others pretend to weep, and make her gravity the subject of their merriment. Perhaps, in a moment of extreme embarrassment, she has committed some breach of good breeding, or looked awkward, or spoken foolishly: she finds afterwards that watchful eyes have been upon her, and that her every tone and movement have been the subject of ridicule in a little coterie of her sisters and her friends. Above all, perhaps she has gone a little too far in meeting the attentions of the other sex, and a merciless outcry is against her, with her sisters at its head.

Besides all this, there are often the strong wills of both parties set in opposition to each other, with a pertinacity that time itself is unable to subdue. For if, from the necessity of circumstances, one sister has on one occasion been compelled to give way, she is only fortified with fresh resolution for the next point of dispute, that she may enjoy her turn of victory and triumph. These disputes are often about the merest trifles in the world, things so entirely worthless and unimportant in themselves, that to find they have been the cause of angry words or bitter feelings, may well excite our astonishment, at the same time that it ought to teach us fresh lessons of distrust of ourselves, of humility, and watchful care.

It is in this manner that sisters will sometimes imbitter their early days, and make what ought to be the bower of repose, a scene of rivalry and strife. But let us change this harsh picture, and turn to the sunnier hours of youthful love, when sisters who have shared one home in childhood, then separated by adverse circumstances, return, after the lapse of years, to enjoy a few brief days of heart-communings beneath the same roof again. How lovely then are the morning hours, when they rise with the sun, to lengthen out the day. They seat themselves in the old window, where their little childish hands were wont to pluck the tendrils of the rambling vine. They look out upon the lawn, and it is arrayed in the same green as when they gambolled there. The summer apple-tree, from whence they shook the rosy fruit, has moss upon its boughs: and the spreading ash reminds them they are no longer able to climb its topmost branch. What vicissitudes have they known—what change of place and circumstance have they experienced—since they planted the small osier that now stands a stately willow by the stream! We will not ask what cruel necessity first drove them separately from this peaceful abode—what blight fell on their prospects—what ruin on their hopes. Are they not sisters unchanged in their affection? —and in this very consciousness they have a world of wealth. Where is the keen, contemptuous gaze of satire now? Where are the bickerings, the envyings, the words of provocation? They would esteem it sacrilege to profane that place and hour with other thoughts than those of kindness. The mote and the beam have vanished from their eyes: they know each other's faults, but they behold them only to pity and forgive, or speak of them only to correct. Each heart is laid bare before the others, and the oil and the wine are poured in, to heal the wounds which the stranger has made. Each has her own store of painful experience to unfold; and she weeps to find her sister's greater than her own. Each has had her share of insult, coldness, and neglect; and she is roused to indignation by hearing that her sister has had the same. Self becomes as nothing in comparison with the intense interest excited by a sister's experience; and as the secret anxieties of each bosom are revealed, fresh floods of tenderness are called forth, and the early bond of childhood, strengthened by vicissitude and matured by time, is woven yet more closely around the hearts of all. Thus they go forth into the world again, strong in the confidence of that unshaken love which formed the sunshine of their childhood, and is now the solace of their riper years. They may weep the tears of the alien in the stranger's home, but they look forward to the summer-days of heart-warm confidence, when they shall meet again with the loveliest and the most beloved of all earth's treasures, and the wintry hours pass over them bereft of half their power to blight.

If such be the experience, and such the enjoyments of sisters separated by affliction, what must be the privileged lot of those, who, without any change of fortune, any falling off from the golden promise of early life, or any heart-rending bereavement, learn the happy art of finding their enjoyment in each other, by studying what will make each other happy? There may be faithful friendships formed in after years; but where a sister is a sister's friend, there can be none so tender, and none so true. For a brother she may possibly entertain a more romantic attachment, because the difference in their circumstances may afford more to interest their feelings; but there is one universal point of failure in the friendship that exists between brothers and sisters—when a man marries, he finds in his wife all that he valued in his sister, with a more endearing sense of certainty in its possession; and when a woman marries, she finds all that she needed in the way of friendship and protection, with more of tenderness, of interest, and identity, than it was possible for her to experience in the affection of her brother. Hence there arises, even in the uncalculating breast of youth, a suspicion that this friendship cannot last; and the breaking up of those establishments in which the sister has regulated the domestic affairs of her brother, is often a melancholy proof that the termination of their intimacy ought to have been calculated upon with more certainty than it generally is.

With sisters the case is widely different. They may seek in vain, through all the high and noble attributes of man, for that which is to be found alone in the true heart of woman; and, weak themselves, susceptible, dependent, and holding their happiness as it were with a sword suspended above their heads, they have need to be faithful to each other.

No friend in after life can know so well as a sister what is the peculiar and natural bias of the character. Education may change the manners, and circumstances may call new faculties to light; but the old leaven remains at the heart's core, and a sister knows it well.

Women often share with other friends enjoy- ments in which their sisters take no part; but they have not roamed together over that garden whose very weeds are lovely—the fertile and luxuriant garden of childhood; they have not drank together at that fountain whose bubbling waters are ever bright and pure—the early fountain of domestic joy; and the absence of this one charm in their friendship, must necessarily shut them out from participation in a world of associations, more dear, more beautiful, and more enduring, than the longest after-life can supply.

I know not how it is with others, but it seems to me, that there never is—there never can be, amusement so original, so piquant, and so fraught with glee, as that which is enjoyed amongst happy sisters at their own fireside, or in their chamber, where one hardly would deny them all their idle hours of laughter and delight. The very circumstances which to one alone would have been a burden of heavy care, when participated in, are nothing; and the mere fact of talking over all their daily trials, sets every bosom free to beat and bound with a new life.

We must not however forget, it is in seasons of affliction that we prove the real value of the deep well-spring of a sister's love. Other hands, and hands perhaps as skilful, may smooth our couch in sickness. Other voices may speak words of kindness in our hour of need, and other eyes may beam upon us with tenderness and love; but can they ever be like the hands that joined with ours in twining the rosy wreaths of infancy—the voices that spoke sweetly to us in the tones of childhood—the eyes that gazed with ours, in all the wonder of first-dawning thought, abroad upon the beautiful creation, over the earth and sea, the green hills, and the waving woods, and up to the starry heavens, that page of glory too bright for human eye to read.

No; there is something in the home-fellowship of early life, that we cannot, if we would, shake off in the days of darkness and distress, when sickness clouds the brow, and grief sits heavily upon the heart. It is then that we pine for the faithful hand, the voice that was an echo to our own, and the kindred countenance so familiar in our childhood; and sisters who are kindly affected one towards another are not slow to answer this appeal of nature. Tender and delicate women are not backward to make sacrifices in such a cause. They will hasten upon difficult and dangerous journeys, without feeling the perils they undergo. The anticipated accidents of time and chance have no weight with them, for self is annihilated by the overwhelming power of their affection. Obstacles cannot hinder, nor persuasion retard their purpose: a sister suffers, and they esteem it their highest privilege to assert, in defiance of all opposition, the indisputable claims of a sister's love. They have an inalienable right to share in her calamity, whatever it may be; and this right they will not resign to another.

But what shall stay my pen, when I touch upon this fertile and inexhaustible theme? Sisters who have never known the deepest, holiest influence of a sister's love, will not be enabled, from any definition I can offer, to understand the purity, and the refreshing power of this well-spring of human happiness. Sisters who have known this, will also know that its height and its depth are beyond

115

the power of language to describe; that it is, indeed, the love which many waters cannot quench, neither can the floods drown it.

Is it not, then, worth all the cost of the most studious consideration, the most careful kindness, to win this treasure, and to make it ours? to purchase this gem, and to wear it next our hearts? I have pointed out some of the means by which it may be lost or won: I will now point out the most important reasons why it should be cherished with unceasing assiduity.

Sisters have an almost unbounded influence over each other; and all influence implies a proportionate degree of moral responsibility. The tone and temper of the human mind must be closely watched, and intimately studied, in order to apply with effect the means of benefit. The most zealous endeavours to do good, may fail for want of opportunity; but opportunity never can be wanting to those who share the same domestic hearth, who sit at the same board, and occupy the same chamber of rest. There must, with such, be unveilings of the heart before each other. There must be seasons for administering advice, and for imparting instruction, which the stranger never can command. But without the practice of those habits of kindness and consideration, so earnestly recommended here, the nearest relative, even the sister, may be placed on the same footing as the stranger, and have no more familiar access to the heart than the mere acquaintance.

It is therefore most important to the true Christian, whose desire is to invite others to a participation in the blessings she enjoys, that she should seek to promote the happiness of those around her, in such a way as to render them easy and familiar in her presence, and to convince them that she is in word and deed their friend. Until this object is attained, little good can be done in the way of influence; but this secured, innumerable channels are opened, by which an enlightened mind may operate beneficially upon others.

We will imagine the case of a sister, whose feelings have been recently impressed with the importance of some hitherto unpractised ditty, and who, at a loss how to begin with that improvement in her daily conduct which conscience points out as necessary to her peace, shrinks from the notice of the world, abashed at the idea of assuming more than she has been accustomed to maintain. With what fear and trembling will such a one, in her closet or her chamber, at the close of the summer's evening, or by the last glimmer of the winter's fire,

116

when she and her sister share the silent hours of night together, unfold the burden of her spirit, and reveal the inner workings of her troubled mind! What should we say of a sister who treated this confidence with treachery, with ridicule or spleen? What should we say, but that she deserved to find the heart she had thus insulted a sealed book to her for ever? What should we say, on the other hand, of her who met this confidence with tenderness and respect? That she enjoyed one of the greatest privileges permitted us in this our imperfect and degraded state—the privilege of imparting consolation and instruction at the same time, and of binding to her bosom the fond affection of a sister, as her comfort and support through all her after years.

It is a common remark for sisters to make upon each other, that they would have paid some deference to the religious scruple, or the pious wish, had it originated with a more consistent person. They should remember that there must be a dawning of imperfect light, to usher in the perfect day; and that he who crushes the first germ of vegetation, commits an act equivalent to that of him who fells the stately tree. They should remember also, it is not only the great and public efforts of christian benevolence and charity, that are owned of God, and blessed with his approval; but that at the hour of midnight, in the secret chamber, and when the world takes no cognizance of our actions, His eye beholds them, and His ear is open to detect the slightest whisper that conveys its blessing or its bane to the heart of a familiar friend.

CHAPTER IX. DOMESTIC HABITS—CONSIDERATION AND KINDNESS.

THERE yet remain some aspects of human life, which it is impossible to pass over without the most earnest solicitude, that even if in all other capacities woman should forget her responsibility, she might remember what is due from her in these. It is, then, to the sacred and inalienable bond between a daughter and her parents, that our attention must now be given.

It would seem but reasonable to suppose, that as soon as an amiable young woman of even partially enlightened mind, attained that stage of maturity when most rational beings begin to make use of their own powers of observation, she would naturally be led to reflect upon the situation of her mother, to contemplate her character and habits, and to regard, with sympathy at least, the daily and hourly fatigues, and anxieties, which the nature of her domestic circumstances renders it necessary for her to undergo. If the young person has brothers or sisters less advanced in life than herself, she cannot fail to observe the assiduity with which all their wants are provided for by maternal care, as well as the self-denial and disinterested love, by which their safety is guarded, and their happiness preserved.

It is equally reasonable to suppose, that having such interesting subjects of grateful and affectionate consideration continually present to her eye, and to her mind, the young person would reason thus: "In this manner my mother has watched over me. Through long nights of weariness and exhaustion she has rocked me in her arms, and stilled the sighs of her own bosom, from the fear of disturbing my repose. Not only has she denied herself every amusement and every gratification that would have drawn her away from the sphere of my childish pastimes, but also the wonted recreations necessary for the preservation of her health; until her cheek grew pale, and her step feeble in my service. I was then unable to make any other return than by my infantine caresses; and often when she was the most weary, or the most enfeebled, my pampered selfishness was the most requiring. Thus I have incurred a debt of gratitude, for the repayment of which the limit of a natural life will scarcely be sufficient. The summer of her existence is waning: mine is yet to come. I will so cultivate my feelings, and regulate my habits, as to enjoy the happiness of sharing her domestic burdens, and thus prove to her that I am not unmindful of the benefit I have myself derived from the long-suffering of a mother's love. "

Do we find this to be the prevailing feeling amongst the young ladies of the present day? Do we find the respected and venerated mother so carefully cherished, that she is permitted to sit in perfect peace, the presiding genius, as she ought to be, over every department of domestic comfort? her cares lightened by participation with her affectionate daughters, her mind relieved of its burdens by their watchful love, herself arrayed in the best attire, as a badge of her retirement from active duty, and smiling as the steps of time glide past her, because she knows that younger feet are walking in her own sweet ways of pleasantness and peace.

Is this the picture presented in the present day by the far-famed homes of England? Do we not rather find the mother, the faithful and time-worn mother of the family, not only the moving spring of all domestic management, but the actual working power, by which every household plan is carried into practical effect. I refer of course to cases where domestics are few, and pecuniary means not over-abundant, where we see the mother hastening with anxious solicitude to answer every call from every member of the family; as if her part in the duties of life was not only to have waited upon her children in infancy, but to conduct them to an easy and luxurious old age; in short, to spare their feet from walking, their hands from labour, and their heads from thought.

I know that it is mistaken kindness in the mother to allow herself thus to become a household drudge. I know also that young ladies are easily satisfied with what appears to them a reasonable excuse, that "mamma prefers doing all these things herself, " that she is such a dear kind soul, they would not rob her even of the merit of mending their own garments. " But let me ask how often she prefers doing these things herself, simply because of their unwillingness to do them; and how their ungracious manner, when they have been asked to relieve her, has wounded her patient spirit, and rendered it less irksome to her to do the hardest manual labour, than to ask them again? Let me remind them also, that there is a habit of doing things so awkwardly, that you will not be likely to be called upon for your services a second time; and whether by accident or design, I will not presume to say, but some young ladies certainly appear to be great adepts in this method of performing their duties.

It is a most painful spectacle, in families where the mother is the drudge, to see the daughters elegantly dressed, reclining at their ease, with their drawing, their music, their fancy-work, and their light reading; beguiling themselves of the lapse of hours, days, and weeks, and never dreaming of their responsibilities; but, as a necessary consequence of the neglect of duty, growing weary of their useless lives, laying hold of every newly invented stimulant to rouse their drooping energies, and blaming their fate, when they dare not blame their God, for having placed them where they are.

These individuals will often tell you with an air of affected compassion—for who can believe it real? —that "poor dear mamma is working herself to death." Yet no sooner do you propose that they should assist her, than they declare she is quite in her element—in, short, that she would never be happy if she had only half as much to do.

I have before observed, that it is not difficult to ascertain, on entering a family, whether the female members of it are, or are not actuated by habits of kindness and consideration; and in no instance is it more easily detected, than in the behaviour of the daughters to their mother. We have probably all seen elegant and accomplished young ladies doing the honours of the house to their guests, by spreading before them that lavish profusion of books and pictures, with which every table of every drawing-room is, in these modern times, adorned. We have heard them expatiate with taste and enthusiasm upon the works of art, upon the beauties of foreign scenery, and the delights of travelling abroad; while the mother is simultaneously engaged in superintending the management of the viands about to be spread before the company, or in placing the last leaf of garniture around the dessert, upon which her daughters have never condescended to bestow a thought.

It is easy, in these cases, to see by the anxious and perturbed appearance of the mistress of the house, when she does at last appear, that she has had no assistance, but that which a very limited number of domestics could render, behind the scenes; that every variety of the repast which her guests are pressed to partake of, has cost her both trouble to invent and labour to prepare; and we feel that we are regaling ourselves too much at her expense.

There is a painful contrast between the care and anxiety depicted on her brow, and the indifference—the real or pretended ignorance with which the young ladies speak, when it is absolutely necessary, of any of those culinary compositions which they regard as belonging exclusively to the department of mothers and servants. If by any possible mischance, the good woman alludes to the flavour of her compounds, wishing, purely for the sake of her guests, that she had added a little more of the salt, or the cinnamon, —indications of nausea, accompanied by symptoms of indignation and disgust, immediately manifest themselves amongst the young ladies, and they really wonder what mamma will be absurd enough to say next.

It is in such families as this, not only on days of leisure, but on days when extra services are sure to be wanted in the home department, that the daughters always find some pressing call upon their attention out of doors. They have their morning calls to make; and there is that mysterious shopping to attend to, that never has an end. Indeed, one would almost think, from the frequency with which they resort to some of the most fashion- able shops in town, that each of these young ladies had a peculiar taste for the mode of life prevailing in this particular sphere of exertion, were it not for the indignation she manifests at the remotest hint upon the duty of assisting her father in his.

It is astonishing how duties out of doors accumulate upon persons who are glad of any excuse to escape from those at home. No one can deny the necessity they are under of pursuing that course of mental improvement begun at school; and there are lectures on every science to be attended, borrowed books to be returned, and little coteries of studious young people, to join in their morning classes.

It is also curious to observe that these young ladies who can with difficulty be induced to move about in their own homes, even to spare their mother's weary feet, who esteem it an act of oppression in her to send them to the highest apartment of the house, and of degradation in themselves, to descend to the lowest, —it is curious to observe how these regard themselves as under an absolute necessity to walk out every day for their health, and how they choose that precise time for walking, when their mothers are most busy, and their domestic peace, by a natural consequence, most likely to be invaded.

I would touch, with extreme delicacy, upon another branch of public occupation, because I believe it to be entered upon, in innumerable instances, with feelings which do honour to humanity, and to that religion, under whose influence alone, such avocations can be faithfully carried on. But I must confess, there appears to me some ground to fear, that the amusement of doing public good, the excitement it produces, and especially the exemption it purchases from domestic requirements, has something to do with the zeal evinced by some young females to be employed as instruments in the dissemination of religious knowledge, and the augmentation of funds appropriated to benevolent uses.

Fearing, however, lest what might assume even the faintest colouring of uncharitableness, should fall from my pen on this delicate but most important subject, I will leave it with the individuals thus engaged, as fitter for their consideration, than for my remark. The world takes cognizance of their actions, and it is perhaps occasionally too lavish in its bestowment of their praises. But the world is a false friend, for it can applaud where there is little real merit, and condemn where there ought to be no blame.

Let not the really faithful and sincere be hurt by these insinuations. Their cause is beyond the penetration of man, and their real springs of action are known, where alone they can be truly estimated, — where alone they can meet with their just reward.

How different from the feelings called forth by habits such as I have just described, are those with which we take up our abode in a family, where we know that the morning sun has risen upon daughters, who meet its early beams with the cheerful determination, that whatever may be the business of the day, their hands, and not their mother's, shall do the actual work. Her experience, and her ever-guiding judgment, may direct their labours; but she who has so often toiled and watched for them, shall at least enjoy another opportunity of seeing how gladly and how richly they can repay the debt. The first thought that occupies their mind, is, how to guard her precious health. They meet her in the morning with affectionate solicitude, and look to see if her cheek has become less pale; whether her smile is languid, or cheerful—her step weary, or light.

I must again repeat, that one of the surest tests of true disinterested love, is this readiness to detect indisposition. Persons who are in the habit of cherishing antipathies, seldom believe in the minor ailments of those they dislike. These facts render it the more surprising, that daughters should not always see the symptoms of exhausted strength, which too frequently manifest themselves in industrious and care-taking mothers; that they should not watch with the tenderest anxiety the slightest indication of their valuable health being liable to decay. Yet so it is, that the mother of a family, who cares for every ailment in her household, is the last to be cared for herself, except in cases affording those beautiful exemplifications of filial duty, to which allusion has just been made.

With daughters who are sensible of the strong claims of a mother's love, no care can be too great, no solicitude too tender, to bestow upon that beloved parent. They know, that if deprived of this friend of their infancy—this guide of their erring feet—the world will be comparatively poor to them: and as the miser guards his hoarded treasure, they guard the life, for which that world would be incapable of supplying a substitute.

There are few subjects of contemplation more melancholy, than the waste of human love which the aspect of this world presents—of deep, tender, untiring, disinterested love, bestowed in such a manner as meets no adequate return; and what must be the harvest gathered in, to a mother's faithful bosom, when she finds that she has reared up children who are too refined to share her humble cares, too learned and too clever to waste their talents on a sphere of thought and action like her own, and too much engaged in the pursuit of intellectual attainments, even to think of her!

Yet to whom do we look for consolation when the blight of sickness or sorrow falls upon our earthly peace, but to a mother! And who but a mother is invited to partake of our afflictions or our trials? If the stigma of worldly degradation falls upon us, we fly to a mother's love for that mantle of charity which is denied elsewhere. With more honoured and distinguished associates, we may have smiled away the golden hours of life's young prime; but the bitter tears of experience are wept upon a mother's bosom. We keep for our summer friends the amusing story, the brilliant witticism, or the intellectual discourse; but we tell to a mother's ear the tale of our distress, and the history of our wrongs. For all that belongs to the weakness and the wants of humanity, a mother's affection is sorely taxed; why then should not daughters have the noble feeling to say before the world, and to let their actions speak the same language, — "This is my earliest, and my best friend. "

It is true, the mother may be far behind the daughter in the accomplishments of modern education; she may, perhaps, occasionally betray her ignorance of polite literature, or her want of acquaintance with the customs of polished society. But how can this in any way affect the debt of obligation existing between her daughter and herself? or how can it lessen the validity of her claim to gratitude for services received, and esteem for the faithfulness with which those services have been performed?

Let us not believe of the young ladies of the present day that they can for any lengthened period, allow the march of mind to outrun the growth of their kindly feelings. Let us rather hope the time is coming when they will exhibit to the world that beautiful exemplification of true dignity—a high degree of intellectual culture rendered conducive to the happiness of those who claim their deepest gratitude and their tenderest affection.

The next view we propose to take of the domestic habits of the women of this favoured country, is that of their behaviour in the relation between daughters and fathers.

The affection existing between fathers and daughters, is a favourite theme with writers both of romance and reality; and the familiar walks of life, we doubt not, are rich in instances of this peculiar kind of affection, existing in a lovely, and most unquestionable form. Still there are points of view in which this subject, as illustrated by the customs of society in the present day, cannot be contemplated without pain.

I have often had occasion to speak of the duties of women towards their fathers, brothers, husbands, and sons, when engaged in the active pursuits of trade; and there is an anomaly presented by society of this class in England, which I am particularly anxious to point out to the rising generation.

There are vast numbers of worthy and industrious men, not only of the young and the middle-aged, but of those who are sinking into the vale of years, who spend almost the whole of their waking lives in scenes and occupations, from which almost everything in the shape of enjoyment must necessarily be shut out.

In looking into the shops, the warehouses, the offices, and the counting-houses, of our commercial and manufacturing towns, we are struck with the destitution of comfort which everywhere prevails, and we ask, —"Are these the abodes of free-born, independent men? "

I should be sorry to be weak enough to suppose that an honest and industrious man may not be just as happy when he treads on boards, as when be treads on Turkey carpets; yet again, when we begin the early day with such individuals, and see what their occupations actually are, from nine in the morning, often until late in the afternoon or evening, for weeks, and months, and years, with scarcely any respite or relaxation, we naturally ask how are the wives and daughters of these men employed? For surely if there be a necessity for the father of the family to be situated thus, the kinder and more disinterested members of his household must be dwelling in abodes even more uncongenial and revolting than these. It is but reasonable to expect that we should find them in apartments less luxurious in their furniture, with windows less pervious to the light of day, their persons perched upon harder stools, and altogether accommodated in an inferior manner. And this we are led to expect, simply because it is difficult to believe of generous-hearted women, that they would be willing to enjoy indulgences purchased at the sacrifice of the comfort of those they love, and by the degradation of those whom they look up to as their superiors.

Perhaps we are told that to man it is no sacriflee to spend his life in these dungeon-like apartments, shut in from the pure air, and compelled to deal with the extreme minutiæ of what is neither interesting nor dignified in itself—that he regards not these trifling inconveniences, that he is accustomed to them, and that they are what the world esteems as manly and befitting; yet on being invited to pay our respects to the ladies of the family, we find ourselves transported into a scene so entirely different from that of his daily toil, that we are led to exclaim, —"How opposite must be the tastes of men and women in this sphere of life, in England! " A little more acquaintance with their domestic habits, however, enables us to discover that their tastes are not so different as their circumstances, and that the cares, the anxieties, and the actual labour, which the man is undergoing every day, are placing him on a very different footing, with regard to personal comfort, from the females of his household.

And how do the women strive to soothe these cares, to relieve these anxieties, and to lighten these labours? Do they not often make their own personal expenses extend to the extreme limit that his means will afford? Do they not dress, and visit, receive visiters, and practise all those elegant accomplishments, which their father's exertions have been taxed to pay for?

I know that the blame does not always rest with the female members of the family, but that men, especially when they first marry, are often pleased to behold their wives arrayed in the most costly habiliments which their means can procure; in addition to this, they believe that their interest in the world is advanced by keeping up a certain degree of costly display, both in dress and furniture. As time advances, however, and their spirits grow less buoyant under the pressure of accumulated cares, especially if these cares have been unproductive of so golden a harvest as they had anticipated, and when daughters are growing up to double—nay, to treble their mother's expenditure, by adding all the imagined essentials of modern refinement; the father then perceives, perhaps too late to retrieve his ruined circumstances, the error into which he has been led; and fain would he then, in the midst of his bitter regrets, persuade his daughters to begin to think and act upon different principles, from those which he has himself so thoughtlessly instilled.

Perhaps the father is sinking into the vale of years, his spirit broken, and some of the growing infirmities of age stealing insidiously upon him. His manly figure begins to stoop, his eye grows dim, and he comes home weary from his daily labour. What a melancholy picture is presented by the image of such a man going forth in public, with his gaily and expensively-dressed daughters fluttering by his side!

Nor is this all. Let us follow them home. He rises early, wearied and worn as he is, and, snatching a hasty breakfast before his daughters have come down, goes forth to his daily avocations, leaving them to their morning calls, light reading, and fancy-work, until his return. At the close of the day, his step is again heard on the threshhold. He has begun to feel that the walk is too much for him. Conveyances, in countless numbers, have passed him on his way, but these are not times for him to afford the luxury of riding, for a rival tradesman has just opened a tempting establishment in the neighbourhood of his own, and the evils of competition are destroying half his gains. With a jaded look and feeble step, then, he enters his home. He wipes the gathering dew from his wrinkled forehead, sits down with a sigh almost amounting to a groan of despondency, and then looks round upon the well-furnished parlour, where the ladies of his family spend their idle hours.

We will not libel the daughters so far as to say, they are guilty of neglect in not inviting him to partake of his evening meal. They may even press their kisses on his cheek, and express their welcome in the warmest terms. Supposing they have done all this, and that he is beginning to feel invigorated and refreshed, perhaps revived a little in his spirit by this evidence of their affection, at length he smiles; and that smile has been eagerly watched for, as the indication that his heart is warming into generosity.

Now is the auspicious time: "Papa, dear, have you ever thought again of the silk cloaks you promised us, as soon as Mr. Moody's bill was paid? And Emma wants a velvet bonnet this winter. And Papa, dear, where did you say we could get the best satin shoes? " "My love, " says the wife, in a graver, and more important tone, "these poor girls are sadly in want of drawing-paper—indeed, of pencils, and of every thing belonging to their drawing; for you know it is of no use having a master to teach them, unless we provide them with the necessary materials. And Isabella's music—I was positively ashamed to hear her play those old pieces again at Mrs. Melburn's last night. "

We have seen pictures of birds of prey hovering about their dying victim; but I doubt whether a still more repulsive and melancholy picture might not be made, of a man of business, in the decline of life, when he naturally asks for repose, spurred and goaded into fresh exertions, by the artificial wants and insatiable demands of his wife and daughters.

The root of the evil, I grant to be, not so much in the hard hearts of the individuals here described, as in the system of false refinement which now prevails in this country. But whatever the cause or its remedy may be, those will be happy days for England, when her noble-minded women, despite the prejudices of early education, shall stand forth before the world, and show that they dare to be dutiful daughters rather than ladies of fashion; and that the principles of integrity, generosity, and natural feeling, have taught them never to wish for enjoyment purchased by the sacrifice of a father's health, or a husband's peace.

I know not whether it often occurs to the young, or only to those whose experience has been of longer duration, to make this observation upon human nature—that it is not intentional offence, or intentional injury, which always inflicts the severest pain. A mother who, by her ill-judged indulgence, fosters in her child a selfish and domi- neering temper, and thus renders such evil dispositions identified with the very nature of that child, so that it is a stranger to any other principles of action, is as much hurt, when in after life, her child is selfish and domineering towards herself, as if he actually departed from his accustomed line of conduct, for the purpose of being pointedly unkind to her. In the same way, the father who has brought up his family in habits of extravagance, when he feels the tide of prosperity turning against him, forgets that those habits are necessarily stronger than his reasoning, and is wounded to the soul to think that his daughters are not more considerate. Upon the same principle of groundless expectation, we often see well-meaning but injudicious parents taking extreme pains to guard their children against one particular error in conduct, or one species of vice, yet neglecting to lay that only sure foundation of moral conduct which is to be found in religious principle; and these, again, are shocked to find, as their children advance in life, that all their endeavours have been unproductive of the desired result. Nor must I, while pointing out errors in the behaviour of children towards their parents, omit to observe, that if parents would be more solicitous to instil into their minds the importance of relative and social duties faithfully performed, instead of captiously reproving them for every deviation from the strict line of these duties, they would find themselves more happy in their families, more tenderly watched over in sickness and sorrow—more cherished and revered in the decline of life.

Still, though the fault may, in some cases, have been originally with the parents, there is little excuse for daughters who are of age to think and act for themselves. Habit, we know, is proverbially accounted second nature; but we know also, that even our first nature is capable of being changed.

He who has become subject to a painful and dangerous disease, through the neglect or mismanagement of those who had the care of him in early life, does not content himself with saying it was the maltreatment of his nurse that brought upon him this calamity. If the disease admits of remedy, if it even admits of alleviation, he is as earnest in seeking out and applying the proper means of relief, as if he had been the sole cause of his own affliction. And shall we confine our powers of reasoning rightly, and acting promptly, to the promotion of the benefit of the body, and leave the immortal mind to suffer for eternity, without applying such remedies as are provided for its use?

Whether the evil be in the original taint of our own nature, or in the same nature inherent in another form, and operating upon us through the medium of injudicious treatment, we stand in precisely the same position with regard to moral responsibility, and accountability to the Searcher of all human hearts.

It is right that the tender sympathy of our friends should be excited, when we tell them, that the faults for which they blame us, were fostered and encouraged by the mistaken judgment of our parents in early life; but there is a tribunal at which this plea will be of little avail, if, while the means of reformation are yet within our reach, we suffer such habits to strengthen and establish themselves as parts of our character; and I would earnestly recommend to the young women of England, that they should rouse themselves, and act upon the first conviction, that the advantages resulting from what is called a finished education, are but so many additional talents lent them, for employment in the service of that gracious Father, who has charged his children with the keeping of each other's happiness; and who, when he instituted the parental bond, and filled the mother's heart with love, and touched with tenderness the father's firmer soul, was pleased to appoint them after years of weakness, suffering, and infirmity, when their children would be able to enjoy the holy privilege of conducting their feeble steps, in peace and safety, towards the close of their earthly pilgrimage.

CHAPTER X. DOMESTIC HABITS—CONSIDERATION AND KINDNESS.

THAT branch of the subject upon which I am now entering, being one of so much importance in the sum of human happiness, as scarcely to admit of comparison with any other, it might be expected that I should especially direct the attention of the reader to the duties of consideration and kindness in the married state, by entering into the minutiæ of its especial requirements, and recommending them, with all the earnestness of emphatic detail, to the serious consideration of the women of England. Happy indeed should I be to do this, did I not feel that, at the same time, I should be touching upon a theme too delicate for the handling of an ordinary pen, and venturing beyond that veil, which the sacredness of such a connexion is calculated to draw over all that is extreme in the happiness or misery of human life.

I shall therefore glance only upon those points which are most obvious to the eye of a third party; and in doing this, it will be found, that many of the remarks I have made upon the behaviour of daughters to their fathers, are equally applicable to that of wives towards their husbands. There is, however, this great difference—the connexion existing between married people is almost invariably a matter of choice. A daughter may, sometimes, imagine herself excused, by supposing that her father is too uncongenial in mind and character, for her to owe him much in the way of companionship. She may think his manners vulgar, and believe that if she had a father who was a gentleman, she would be more attentive and considerate to him: but her husband cannot have married her without her own consent; and therefore the engagement she has voluntarily entered into, must be to fulfil the duties of a wife to him as he is, not as she could have wished or imagined him to be.

These considerations lead me to a view of the subject which I have often been compelled to take with deep regret, but which I fear no human pen, and still less mine, will be able to change—it is the false system of behaviour kept up between those who are about to enter into the rela- tion of marriage; so that when they settle down upon the true basis of their own characters, and appear to each other what they actually are, the difference is sometimes so great, as almost to justify the inquiry, whether the individual can really be the same.

I presume not to expatiate upon that process denominated courtship, as it is frequently carried on by men. I venture not to accuse them of injustice, in cherishing, in their early intercourse with the object of their choice, the very faults which they afterwards complain of in the wife. My chief solicitude is for my own sex, that they should not only be faithful after marriage, but upright and sincere before; and that they should scorn to engage a lover, by little acts of consideration and kindness, which they are not prepared to practise even more willingly towards the husband.

I have known cases in which a kind-hearted woman would have esteemed herself robbed of a privilege, if her lover had asked any other person than herself so much as to mend his glove. Yet is it not possible for the same woman, two years after marriage, to say—"My sister, or my cousin, will do that for you. I am too busy now. "

Nor is it the act alone, but the manner in which the act is done, that conveys a false impression of what will be the manner of that woman after marriage. I charge no one with intentional deception. The very expression of the countenance is that of real and intense enjoyment, while the act of kindness is performed. All I regret is, that the same expression of countenance should not always accompany the same performance in the wife. Women of acute sensibility must feel the loss of personal attractions, when time begins to tell upon their youthful charms. But, oh! that they would learn by the warning of others, rather than by their own experience, that it is more frequently the want of this expression of cheerful, genuine, disinterested kindness, than the want of youthful beauty, that alienates their husbands' love, and makes them objects of indifference, or worse.

The cultivation of acquaintance before marriage, with a view to that connexion taking place, for the most part goes but a very little way towards the knowledge of real character. The parties usually meet in the hey-day of inexperienced youth; and while they exult in the unclouded sunshine of life, their mutual endeavours to please, are rewarded by an equal willingness to be pleased. The woman, especially, is placed in a situation highly calculated to excite the greatest possible degree of complacency. She is treated by a being upon whom she depends, and he most probably her superior, as if she was incapable of error, and guiltless of a single fault. Perhaps she warns him of his mistake, speaks of her own defects, and assures him that she is not the angelic creature he supposes her to be; but she does all this with so sweet a grace, and looks all the while so pleased to be contradicted, that her information goes for nothing; and we are by no means assured that she is not better satisfied it should be so.

If, for instance, she really wishes him to know that her temper is naturally bad, why is she invariably so mild, and bland, and conciliating in his presence? If she wishes him to believe that she has a mind not capable of entering fully into the interest of his favourite books, and the subjects of his favourite discourse, why does she appear to listen so attentively when he reads, and ask so many questions calculated to draw him out into conversation? If she wishes him to suppose that she is not always a lively and agreeable companion, why does she not occasionally assume the tone and manner so familiar to her family at home—answer him shortly, hang down her head, and mope away the evening when he is near her? If she really wishes him to believe her, when she tells him that she is but ill-informed, and wanting in judgment; why, when he talks with her, does she take so much pains to express opinions generally believed to be correct, and especially such as coincide with his own? If she occasionally acts from caprice, and really wishes him to know that she does so, to the injury of the comfort of those around her; why, whenever she practises in this way upon him, does she win him back again, and soothe his feelings with redoubled kindness, and additional solicitude to please.

Perhaps she will tell me she acts in this manner, because it would be unamiable and ungenerous to do otherwise. To which I answer, If it be unamiable and ungenerous to the lover, how much more so must it be to the husband? I find no fault with the sweetness, the irresistible charm of her behaviour before marriage. It is no more than we ought to practise towards those whose happiness is bound up with ours. The falling off afterwards is what I regard as so much to be deplored in the character of woman; for wherever this is observed, it seems to indicate that her mind has been low enough to be influenced by a desire of establishing herself in an eligible home, and escaping the stigma foolishly attached to the situation of an old maid.

I have devoted an earlier CHAPTER in this work to the consideration of dress and manners; but I have omitted one of the most striking points of view in which these subjects can be regarded, —the different characters they sometimes assume before, and after marriage.

When a young lady dresses with a view to general approbation, she is studiously solicitous to observe, what she believes to be, the rules of good taste; and more especially, if a gentleman, whose favourable opinion she values, evinces any decided symptoms of becoming her admirer. She then meets him with her hair arranged in the most becoming style; with the neat shoe, and pure-white gloves, which she has heard him commend in others, with the pale scarf, the quiet-coloured robe, and with the general aspect of her costume accommodated to his taste. He cannot but observe this regard to his wishes, and he notes it down as a proof of amiable temperament, as well as sympathy of habitual feeling. Auguring well for his future happiness with a woman, who even in matters of such trifling moment is willing to make his wish her law, he prevails upon her at last to crown that happiness by the bestowment of her hand.

In the course of three years, we look in upon this couple in the home they are sharing together. We suppose the lady to be the same, yet cannot feel quite sure, her whole appearance is so changed. The hair that used to be so carefully braided, or so gracefully curled, is now allowed to wander in dishevelled tresses, or swept away from a brow, whose defects it was wont to cover. There is a forlornness in her whole appearance, as if she had, not, as formerly, any worthy object for which to study these secondary points of beauty; and we inwardly exclaim how the taste of her husband must have changed, to allow him to be pleased with what is so entirely the opposite of his original choice. On a second observation, however, we ask whether he actually is pleased, for there is nothing like satisfaction in the look with which he turns away from the unbecoming cap, the soiled kerchief, and the neglected aspect of the partner of his life.

If married women, who allow themselves to fall into that state of moral degradation, which such an appearance indicates, feel pained at symptoms of estrangement in their husband's affections, they must at least be satisfied to endure the consequences of their own want of consideration, without sympathy or commiseration. They may, perhaps, feel disposed to say their punishment is too severe for such a fault. They love their husbands as faithfully as ever, and expected from them a love that would have been more faithful in return, than to be shaken by any change in mere personal appearance. But let me tell them, that the change which owes its existence to our own fault, has a totally different effect upon the feelings of a friend, from that which is the consequence of our misfortine; and one of the most bitter and repulsive thoughts that can be made to rankle in a husband's bosom, is, that his wife should only have deemed it necessary to charm his eye, until she had obtained his hand; and that, through the whole of his after life, he must look in vain for the exercise of that kind consideration in consulting his tastes and wishes, that used to lend so sweet a charm to the season of youthful intercourse.

It is a subject well calculated to inspire the most serious regret, that men should practise, throughout the season of courtship, that system of indiscriminate flattery which lulls the better judgment of woman into a belief that she must of necessity be delightful to him—delightful, faults and all—nay, what is infinitely worse than this, into a secret suspicion, that the faults which her female friends have been accustomed to point out, have no existence in reality, and that to one who knows and loves her better, she must appear in her naturally amiable and attractive character. —Could she be persuaded, on that important day, when she is led home from the altar, adorned, attended upon, and almost worshipped—could she be persuaded to cast one impartial glance into her own heart, she would see that the treasure she was bestowing, had many drawbacks from its value, and that all the happiness it was in her power to confer, must necessarily, from the nature or that heart, be accompanied with some alloy.

"Alas! " she would say, after this examination, "he knows me not. Time will reveal to him my secretly cherished faults. " And when this conviction was confirmed through the days and years of her after life, she would esteem it but a small sacrifice of time and patience to endeavour to render herself personally attractive to him. Nay, so grateful would she feel for his charitable forgiveness, that when the evil dispositions inherent in her nature were thrown into more glarihg light, she would esteem it a privilege to be able by the simplest means to convince him, that, with all her faults, she was not so guilty of a disregard to his wishes, as to refuse in these minor points to conform her habits to his taste.

Many of the remarks into which I have been led by a consideration of the subject of dress, are equally applicable to that of manner, as relates to its connexion with social and domestic happiness before and after marriage. We are all aware that neither beauty, nor personal adornment, nor the most brilliant conversation, can be rendered altogether charming to any individual, without the accompaniment of a peculiar kind of manner, by which that individual is made to feel that he partakes in the pleasant thoughts, and kind feelings, of the party whose object it is to please.

Women who possess the tact, to know exactly how to give pleasure, are peculiarly skilled in those earnest looks, and cheerful smiles, and animated responses, which constitute more than half the charm of society. We sometimes see, in social evening circles, the countenance of an intelligent young lady lighted up with such a look of deep and glowing interest, as to render her perfectly beautiful, during the time she is addressed by a distinguished friend, or even an attractive stranger.

I will not say that the same expression is not always worn by the same individual at the domestic hearth, when she listens to the conversation of her husband. I will not so far libel my countrywomen, because I know that there are noble and admirable instances of women who are too diffident and too simple-hearted to study how to shine in public, who yet, from the intensity of their own feelings, the brilliance of their own powers of perception, and the deep delight of listening to the gentle tones of a beloved voice, when it speaks at once to their understanding and their hearts. —I know that such women do wear an aspect of almost spiritual beauty, and speak and act with an almost superhuman grace, when no eye beholds them but that which is most familiar, and which is destined to look upon the same path of life with theirs.

After acknowledging these instances, I must suppose a case; and for the sake of argument imagine what would be the feelings of a husband, who, in mixed society, should see his wife the centre of an animated group—pleased herself, and giving pleasure to all around her—the expression of intense interest depicted on her countenance, and mingled with an apprehension so lively and vivid, as almost to amount to presentiment of every probable turn in the discourse; her eyes lighted up with animation, and her cheeks dimpled over with the play of sunny smiles—what would be the feelings of a husband who should have marked all this, and when at his own fireside he felt the want of pleasant converse to beguile the winter's even- ing of its length, should be answered by that peculiar tone of voice, that depression of countenance, and that forbidding manner, which are more powerful in imposing silence than the most imperative command?

In fact, there is a manner all-powerful in its influence upon domestic happiness, in which there seems to be embodied a spirit of evil too subtle for detection, and too indefinite to be described by any name. It is not precisely a sullen manner, nor, in its strictest sense, a repulsive manner: for the individual who adopts it may be perfectly civil all the while. It does not consist in pointed insult, or, indeed, in any thing pointed. It conveys no reproach, nor suffers the party upon whom it operates to suppose that redress is the thing desired. It invites no explanation, and makes no complaint. Its only visible characteristic is, that the eye is never raised to gaze upon its object, but invariably directed past it, as if that object had no ubiquity—in short, had no existence, and was not required to have any.

This is the manner I should describe as most expressive of natural antipathy without the energy of active dislike; and yet this manner, as before stated, is so potent in its influence, that it seems to lay, as it were, an unseen axe at the root of all domestic confidence; and, difficult as it must necessarily be for a woman to maintain this manner, there have been instances in which it has destroyed a husband's peace, without affording him even the satisfaction of any definite cause of complaint. There are degrees of the same manner practised every day in all classes of society, but never without a baneful effect, in poisoning our kindly feelings, and decreasing the sum of human happiness.

We are all too much disposed to put on what I would describe as company-manners. Not only are our best dresses reserved for our visiters, but our best behaviour too. I have often been struck with the bland smiles that have been put on in welcoming guests, and the appearance of extreme interest with which such guests have been listened to; when, five minutes after their departure, the same subject having been taken up by some unfortunate member of the family, no interest whatever has been elicited, no smile awakened, and scarcely so much as a patient and respectful answer drawn forth. I have observed, also, with what forbearance the absurdities of a stranger have been endured: the twice-told tale, when begun again in company, has apparently been as fresh and entertaining as the first time it was heard. The folly of ignorance has then had no power to disgust, nor the impertinence of curiosity to offend.

When I have marked all this, I have thought, If we could but carry away our company-smiles to the home fireside, speak always in the gentle and persuasive tones made use of in the evening party, and move along the domestic walk with that suavity of manner which characterises our intercourse with what is called society, —how pleasant would those homes become to the friends who look for their hours of refreshment and relaxation there; and how seldom should we have to complain of our companionship being neglected for that of more brilliant circles and more interesting scenes!

In writing on the subject of consideration and kindness before and after marriage, I have purposely confined my remarks to a very slight and superficial view of the subject. The world that lies beyond, I cannot regard as within the province of my pen—I might almost say, within the province of any pen: for such is the difference in human character, and in the circumstances by which character is developed, that it would scarcely be possible to speak definitely of a line of conduct by which the lives of any two married women could properly be regulated, because such conduct must bear strict reference to the habits and temperament of the husband, whose peculiarities of character would have to be taken into account.

I must therefore be satisfied to recommend this wide and important field of contemplation to the serious attention and earnest solicitude of my countrywomen; reminding them, only, before we leave this subject, that if, in the first instance, they are induced by selfish feeling to consult their immediate interest or convenience, they are, in a secondary manner, undermining their own happiness by failing to consult that of the being whose destiny is linked with theirs.

What pen can describe the wretchedness of that woman, who finds herself doomed to live unloved; and to whom can she look for confidence and affection, if shut out from the natural sources of enjoyment at home? There is no loneliness—there can be none, in all the waste or peopled deserts of this world, bearing the slightest comparison with that of an unloved wife? She stands amidst her family like a living statue amongst the marble memorials of the dead—instinct with life, yet paralyzed with death—the burning tide of natural feeling circling round her heart—the thousand channels frozen, through which that feeling ought to flow.

So pitiable, so utterly destitute of consolation is this state, to which many women have reduced themselves by mere carelessness of the common and familiar means of giving pleasure, that I must be pardoned for writing on this subject with more earnestness than the minuteness of its detail would seem to warrant. We may set off in life with high notions of loving, and of being loved, in exact proportion to meritorious desert, as exemplified in great and noble deeds. But on a closer and more experimental view of human life, we find that affection is more dependent upon the minutiæ of every-day existence; and that there is a greater sum of affection really lost, by filtering away through the failure of seeming trifles, than by the shock of great events.

We are apt also to deceive ourselves with regard to the revival of affection after its decay. Much may be done to restore equanimity of mind, to obtain forgiveness, and to be reinstated in esteem; but I am inclined to think, that when once the bloom of love is gone—when it has been brushed away by too rude or too careless a hand, it would be as vain to attempt to restore it, as to raise again the blighted flower, or give wings to the butterfly which the storm had beaten down.

How important is it, then, that women should guard, with the most scrupulous attention, this treasure of their hearts, —this blessing of their homes; and since we are so constituted, that trifles make the sum of human happiness, that they should lose no opportunity of turning these trifles to the best account.

Besides these considerations, there is one awful and alarming fact connected with this subject, which ought to be indelibly impressed upon our minds; it is, that we have but a short time, it may be but a very short time, allowed us for promoting the comfort or the happiness of our fellow-creatures. Even if we ourselves are spared to reach the widest range of human existence, how few of those we love will number half that length of years! Even the hand that is clasped in ours, the eyes that reflect the intelligence of our souls, and the heart that beats an echo to every pulse we feel, may be cold and motionless before to-morrow's sun has set!

Were the secrets of every human bosom laid open, I believe we should behold no darker passage in the page of experience, than that which has noted down our want of kindness and consi- deration to those who are gone before us to another world.

When we realize the agonizing sensation of bending over the feeble frame of a beloved friend, when the mortal conflict is approaching, and the fluttering spirit is about to leave its earthly tenement; and looking back upon a long, dark past, all blotted over with instances of our unkindness or neglect, and forward unto that little span of life, into which we would fain concentrate the deep affection, that, in spite of inconsistencies in our past conduct, has all the while been cherished in our hearts, —with what impassioned earnestness would we arrest the pale messenger in his career, and stay the wings of time, and call upon the impatient spirit to return, to see, and feel, and understand our love.

Perhaps we have been negligent in former seasons of bodily affliction; have not listened patiently to the outpouring of natural feeling, and have held ourselves excused from attendance in the sick-chamber; and there has gone forth that awful sentence, "It is the last time! " the last time we can offer the cordial draught, or smooth the restless pillow, or bathe the feverish brow! And now, though we would search all the treasures of the earth for healing medicine, and rob ourselves of sleep and rest, and sustenance, to purchase for the sufferer one hour of quiet slumber, and pour our tears upon that aching brow, until its burning heat was quenched; —it is in vain, for the eye is glazed, the lips are paralyzed, the head begins to droop, and expiring nature tells us it is all too late!

Perhaps we have not been sympathizing, kind, or tender, in those by-gone years of familiar confidence, when we were called upon to share the burdens of a weary bosom, whose inner feelings were revealed to us, and us alone. Yes, we can remember, in the sunny days of youth, and through the trials of maturer life, when the appeals of affection were answered with fretfulness or captious spleen, when estrangement followed, and we could not, if we had desired it, then draw back the love we had repulsed. And now we hear again that awful sentence—"It is the last time! "—the last time we can ever weep upon that bosom, or lay our hand upon that head, or press a fond, fond kiss upon those closing lips. Fain would we then throw open the flood-gates of our hidden feeling, and pour forth words of more than tenderness. Alas! the once wished-for tide would flow, like the rising surf around a shattered wreck—too late.

Perhaps we have been guilty of a deeper sin against our heavenly Father, and the human family whose happiness he has in some measure committed to our trust. And oh! let the young ask diligently of the more experienced, how they can escape the aching consciousness that may pursue them to the grave, and only then commence the reality of its eternal torment—the consciousness of having wasted all our influence, and neglected all our means of assisting those who were associated with us by the closest ties, in preparing for another and a better world.

Perhaps they once sought our society for the benefit of spiritual communion. Perhaps they would have consulted us in cases of moral difficulty, had we been more gracious and conciliating. Perhaps we have treated lightly the serious scruples they have laid before us, or, what is still more probable, perhaps the whole tenour of our inconsistent lives has been the means of drawing them away from the altar, on which they saw such unholy incense burning. And now, "it is the last time"—the last time we can ever speak to them of eternity, of the state of their trembling souls before the eye of a just and holy God, or raise their fainting hopes to the mercy still offered to their acceptance, through Him who is able to save to the uttermost. Oh! for the trumpet of an archangel, to awake them from the increasing torpor of bodily and spiritual death. Oh! for a voice that would embody in one deep, awful, and tremendous word, all— all for which our wasted life was insufficient! It is in vain that we would call upon the attributes of nature and of Deity to aid us. They are gone! It was the final struggle; and never more will that pale marble form be roused to life by words of hope or consolation. They are gone. The portals of eternity are closed—It is too late.

Let it be a subject of grateful acknowledgment with the young, that to them this fearful sentence has not yet gone forth—that opportunity may still be offered them to redeem the time. They know not, however, how much of this time remains at their disposal; and it might occasionally be some assistance to them in their duties, would they cultivate the habit of thinking, not only of their own death, but of the death of their companions.

There are few subjects more calculated for solemn and affecting thought, than the fact that we can scarcely meet a blooming circle around a cheerful hearth, but one individual at least, in that circle, will be cherishing in her bosom the seeds of some fatal malady.

It is recorded of the Egyptians, that amongst their ancient customs they endeavoured to preserve the salutary remembrance that they were liable to death, by placing at their festal boards, a human skeleton; so that while they feasted, and enjoyed the luxuries of this life, they should find it impossible to beguile themselves into a belief in its perpetual duration.

It is not necessary that we should resort to means so unnatural and repulsive; though the end is still more desirable for us, who are trusting in a better hope, to keep in view. Neither is it necessary that the idea should be invested with melancholy, and associated with depression. It is but looking at the truth. And let us deceive ourselves as we may, the green church-yard with its freshly-covered graves—the passing-bell—the slowly-moving hearse—the shutters closed upon the apartment where the sound of merriment was lately heard—the visitations of disease within our homes—even the hectic flush of beauty—all remind us that the portion of time allotted for the exercise of kindly feeling towards our fellow-creatures, is fleeting fast away; and that to-day, if ever, we must prove to the Great Shepherd of the christian fold, that we are not regardless of that memorable injunction—By this shall all men know that ye are my disciples, if ye have love one to another.

CHAPTER XI. SOCIAL INTERCOURSE OF THE WOMEN OF
ENGLAND—CAPRICE—AFFECTATION—LOVE OF
ADMIRATION.

THE higher admiration we bestow upon the nature and attributes of
any subject of contemplation, the more painful and acute is our
perception of its defects. And thus when we think of woman in her
most elevated character, consider the extent of her capabilities, and
her wonderful and almost unfailing power of being great on great
occasions, we are the more disposed to regret that she has a power
equally unlimited, of making herself little; and that, when indolence
or selfishness is allowed to prevail over her better feelings, this
power is often exercised to the annoyance of society, and to her own
disgrace.

Those who understand the construction of woman's mind, however,
will find some excuse for this, in the natural versatility of her mental
faculties, in the multiplicity of her floating ideas, in the play of her
fancy, and in the constant overflow of her feelings, which must
expend themselves upon some object, either worthy or unworthy;
and which consequently demand the utmost attention to what is
really important, in order that this waste of energy, of feeling, and
emotion, may be avoided.

The word caprice, in its familiar acceptation, is one of very indefinite
signification. I shall endeavour to confine my use of it to those cases
in which the whim of the moment is made the rule of action, without
any reference to right reason, or even to the gratification or
annoyance of others; and I shall endeavour to show, that with regard
to this feminine fault, as well as many others, women are not fairly
dealt with by society.

How often do we see, for instance, a beautiful and fascinating girl
expressing the most absurd antipathies, or sympathies, and acting in
the most self-willed and irrational manner; in short, performing a
part, which, in a plain woman, would be regarded not only as
repulsive, but unamiable in the utmost degree; yet because she is
beautiful, her admirers appear to think all these little freaks of fancy
highly becoming, and captivating in the extreme. If she chooses to
find fault with what all the rest of the company are admiring—how
delightfully peculiar are her tastes! If she will walk out when others
are not disposed for walking—what obsequious attendants she

immediately finds, all ready to say the evening is fine, the air inviting, and the general aspect of nature exactly what she chooses it should be! If she persists in refusing to play a favourite air—what a dear capricious creature she always is! and in this, as well as all other whims, she must be humoured to the extent of her selfishness.

I will not pretend to say that beauty alone can command this influence, though it unquestionably has a power beyond all calculation. The being who thus assumes the right to tyrannize, must have obtained the suffrages of society by the exercise of some particular powers of fascination, which she wants the judgment and good feeling to use for better purposes.

We have seen her, then, a sort of idol in society, the centre of an admiring circle, endowed with the royal privilege of incapability of doing wrong. We have seen her admired, apparently beloved; and we turn to the little coteries of dissentients who are sure to be formed in all companies where a being of this description is found. Amongst these we find that her character is treated, not with justice, though that had been enough, but with the sharp inspection of keen and envious eyes; and we are soon convinced, that if in public she is raised to the distinction of an idol, she is in private most unscrupulously deprived of the honours she was but too willing to assume.

I speak not of this instance, in order to bring forward the want of charity and kindly feeling prevailing in the world. I simply state that such things are, —in order to show that the deference paid to the caprices of women by a few partial admirers, is no real test of the favour they obtain in general society. And if, in such instances where youth and beauty cast their lovely mantle over every defect, woman's faults are still brought to light, what must be her situation—what her treatment by the world, where she has nothing of kind to palliate her weakness, or recommend her to the charity and forbearance of her fellow-creatures.

Caprice, like many other feminine faults, appears almost too trifling in its minutiæ—too insignificant in its detail, to deserve our serious condemnation; yet, if caprice has the power to make enemies, and to destroy happiness, it ought not to be regarded as unimportant in itself. With regard to many other subjects of consideration connected with the virtues or the errors of woman, we have had to observe, that each individual act may be almost beneath our notice in itself, and yet may form a part of such a whole, as the utmost capabilities of human intellect would be unable to treat with justice and effect.

The case is precisely the same with feminine caprice. It is but a slight deviation either from sense or propriety, to choose to differ from the majority of opinions, to choose to do, and to make others do, what is not agreeable to them, or to refuse to do what would give them pleasure. But, when this mode of conduct becomes habitual, when beauty fades, and the idol of society is cast into the shade, when disappointment irritates the temper, and "sickness rends the brow, " and grief sits heavily upon the soul—in these seasons of nature's weakness, when woman's trembling heart is apt to sink within her, to what loneliness and bitterness of experience must she be consigned, if her own indulgence of caprice has driven from her all the friends who might have administered to her consolation in this hour of need.

This view of the subject, however, she is certainly at liberty to take, and, counting the cost, to indulge her momentary wishes at the expense of her future peace. The question of most serious importance, is, how far are we justified in trifling with the happiness, the comfort, or even the convenience of others, for the sake of indulging our own caprices?

I have before stated, that in acting from caprice, we act without reference to common sense, or right feeling. If, therefore, a woman chooses to be capricious, there is no help for it. Argument has no power to convince her that she is wrong, and opposition only strengthens her determination: no matter how many are made to suffer annoyance from her folly, or grief from her perverseness. It is her choice to be capricious, and they must abide by the consequences. Thus she exemplifies—it may be said in actions extremely minute and unimportant—but still she does exemplify, how much mischief may be done by a weak judgment, a selfish temper, and an unenlightened mind.

The domestic habits and social intercourse of the women of England, are peculiarly favourable to the counteraction of the natural tendency to caprice in the female character, because they afford a supply of constant occupation, and invest that occupation with the dignity of moral duty. When, therefore, we find individuals acting from caprice, in the middle classes of English society, we know that it exists in spite of circumstances; and we consequently regard with proportionate condemnation, those who are so far deficient in good taste, and good feeling, as to prefer such a mode of exhibiting their follies to the world.

It might require some degree of philosophical examination, accurately to define the nature and origin of caprice; yet so far as I have been able to ascertain by observations upon society in general, I should be inclined to describe it as arising from the same cause as affectation; and both to owe their existence to a desire to attract attention, or a belief that attention is attracted by what is said or done. Caprice refers more to a weak and vain desire to be important; affectation, to a desire to make ourselves admired. Both are contemptible in the extreme. Yet one is so powerful in provoking the temper, the other in exciting ridicule and disgust, that both are worthy of our careful examination, in order that we may detect the lurking evil wherever it exists in our own conduct.

Affectation is in practice a species of minute deception; in effect, a palpable mockery of that which is assumed. I am aware that it is often the accompaniment of extreme bashfulness and diffidence of self; but this is seldom or never the case, except where there is a secret, yet strong desire, if it were possible, to be the object of admiration to others. Along with affectation, there is generally a prevailing impression of being the object upon which all, or at least many eyes are fixed. For who would be at the trouble of all those distortions of countenance, inflexions of voice, and manoeuvrings of body and limb, which we often observe in company, did they not believe themselves to be "The observed of all observers"?

If by thinking too meanly of ourselves, we are overwhelmed with humiliation in public, and tormented with dissatisfaction in private, it is clear that there is as much vanity and selfishness in this depreciation of our own character, as in the more exalted and comfortable inflation of conceit. The only difference is, —in one case we are piqued and wounded that we cannot be admired; in the other, we believe ourselves to be admired when we are not.

The suffering produced by this kind of vanity, is generally accompanied both with affectation and bashfulness; but we must not suppose, because a blush suffuses the countenance, and the out-stretched hand is seen to tremble, that the individual who is guilty of this breach of fashionable indifference, is necessarily free from vanity, or guiltless of a desire to be admired.

Those who have travelled much, and seen much of the world, are generally cured both of bashfulness and affectation, by one of these two causes, —either they have been so often in company without making any impression, that they have learned of how little importance it is to society in what manner they behave, or how they look; or they have learned a still more useful lesson, that the admiration of man, even in its fullest sense, goes but a little way towards satisfying the heart.

The affectation most frequently detected in the behaviour of women, is that which arises from an inordinate desire of being agreeable. A certain degree of this desire is unquestionably of great service in preserving them from the moral degradation which I have before alluded to, as attaching to personal neglect—as indicating a low state of mind wherever it exists, and procuring a low degree of estimation for the individual who thus allows her negligence to gain the ascendancy over her good taste.

On the other hand, what may with propriety be called an inordinate desire to be admired, when it takes the place of higher motives and principles of action, is perhaps a more fertile source both of folly and of suffering, than any other which operates upon the life and conduct of woman. As exhibited through the single medium of affectation, it is so varied in its character, and so unbounded in its sphere of operation, that to attempt to describe it in detail would require volumes, rather than pages: I shall therefore confine my remarks to that species of affectation which is the most prevalent in the present day.

As the peculiar kind of merit assumed by the hypocrite is, in some measure, a test of what is most popular and most approved in society; so the prevailing affectation of the day, is an indication of the taste of the times—of the general tone of public feeling, and of the tendency of private habits. That which most recommends itself to the acceptance and adoption of the young ladies of the present day, is an affectation of refinement—not refinement of feeling as relates to the means possessed by every human being, of increasing pleasure and alleviating pain, in the circle of friends or relatives by which they are surrounded; but refinement of self, so that the individual who has attained to this degree of elevation, shall be exempt from all personal obligations, particularly such as would render her instrumental in the performance of social and domestic services amongst her fellow-creatures. Women who affect this kind of refinement, are extremely fastidious in all that relates to manual employment. They cannot touch the coarse material that supplies our bodily wants, or constitutes our personal comfort. They loathe the very mention of those culinary compounds, which nevertheless their fair lips condescend to admit; and they shrink with horror from the vulgar notion that the old grandmother-duties of preparing a clean hearth, and a comfortable fireside, for a husband or a brother, could by any possibility devolve upon them.

For this kind of affectation, however, there is some excuse in our natural indolence; and in the exemption it procures from personal exertion; but when we see the absolute pains which some of the same individuals will take to make themselves appear dependent, useless, and wholly inadequate to self-preservation, we are startled with a new idea, and entirely at a loss to account for this phenomenon in human nature.

It is with difficulty I admit the belief that women are in reality the victims of all those foolish fears, with which they profess to be annoyed, and with which they unquestionably are very successful in annoying others. It is with difficulty I admit this belief, because I see—and see with admiration, that some of the most delicate women, the most sensitively alive to impression, and the most susceptible both of pleasure and pain, can, when called upon by duty, and actuated by principle, set all these idle fears aside, and dare to do what man would almost shrink from. I cannot therefore divest myself of all suspicion, that a little of this feminine timidity is sometimes assumed, and a great deal of it encouraged, for the sake of effect—for the sake of making it appear to society that the individual who acts this part, is too refined to have ever been accustomed to the rough usages of common life.

I say this with all charity, and with much compassion for those whose bodily and mental conformation does really render them the victims of causeless fear; and when we see such persons endeavouring to subdue their timidity, ashamed of it as a weakness, and especially solicitous for it not to interfere with the comfort or convenience of others, they justly claim, not only our sympathy, but our admiration. It is the display of terror that I would speak of in terms which can scarcely be too contemptuous—the becoming start, the modulated shriek, the studied appeal for manly protec- tion, and all that elaboration of feminine delicacy, which it sometimes appears to be the business of a life to exhibit.

Besides this kind of affectation, I will mention another species, if possible still more unaccountable in its nature and cause. It is the affectation of ignorance respecting common things. It is by no means unusual with young ladies to appear to plume themselves upon not knowing how any familiar or ordinary thing is made or done. They refuse to understand anything about machinery, and bring into their conversation, what they seem to regard as the most entertaining blunders, whenever conversation turns upon the occupations of the labouring classes. The same individuals seldom know the way to any place, are incapable of discovering whether their faces are turned to the north or the south; and if you ask them with any idea of receiving an answer, from what quarter the wind is blowing, you might as well expect them to tell you whether the tide is at that moment rising in Nootka sound.

If any of these confessions of ignorance, when forced upon them, were attended with embarrassment or shame, they would claim our sisterly compassion; and sorry should I be to make their blushes the subject of public remark. But when we find this ignorance persisted in, made conspicuous on every possible occasion, and attended with "nods, and becks, and wreathed smiles, " as if it were sure to meet with a favourable reception in society, we cannot withhold the exclamation of our patriot poet, that from our souls we "loathe all affectation. "

It is evident that this helplessness, and this ignorance, where they are assumed, must be so for the purpose of attracting attention, claiming assistance, it may be, from the other sex, and establishing an unquestionable claim to refinement, by giving forth to society an idea of habits of exclusion from all vulgar or degrading association.

It is difficult to imagine a mode of life, or a combination of circumstances, less advantageous to the cultivation of such false notions of refinement, than those which are presented by the real situation of the women of England; and it is impossible not to look, with gloomy anticipations for the future welfare of our country, upon the increasing prevalence of these erroneous ideas of what is really excellent and admirable in the female character.

The view we have taken of the subjects at pre- sent under consideration, naturally leads us to that great root of more than half the folly and the misery existing amongst women—the love of admiration.

The extreme case, of a woman totally indifferent to the good opinion of her fellow-creatures, would fail to recommend itself to our regard, inasmuch as it would argue a deficiency in her nature, of those feelings which have been given her as a means of happiness to herself and benefit to others. She would stand amidst her fellow-creatures a lonely and isolated being, living and acting without reference to the existence of any other being; and if she escaped the thousand disappointments of those who act from opposite motives, she would be equally exempt from any claim upon their affection.

Such individuals, however, are so rare, that the consideration of their peculiarities would be a fruitless waste of time and thought. It is to the opposite extreme of character that our attention must now be given. And here I would request the reader to bear in mind, that my remarks refer strictly to the love of admiration, not to the love of approbation, which I take to be a natural and lawful stimulus to all that is excellent in female conduct.

When we look upon human life with "critical inspection, " we find that a vast proportion of the apparent motives acted upon before the world, are not the real motives by which the individual actors are influenced; and that this system of deception is often carried on unconsciously to them, because they are themselves betrayed by the deceitfulness of their own hearts. In no instance is this more strikingly the case than in our love of admiration. To gratify this desire, what suffering are we not willing to endure, what pains do we not take, what patience can we not exercise; and all under the most plausible pretences—pretences that impose upon others less effectually than ourselves, that we are acting upon higher and more praiseworthy principles. There is this difference, however, to be observed between acting from worthy and unworthy motives: when our endeavours are unsuccessful and our motives correct, we seldom give way to the fretfulness of disappointment; but when our endeavours are ineffectual, and we look back into our own hearts, and find them unsupported by any laudable object, our fretfulness is often exasperated into bitterness and spleen.

Observation and experience have taught me to believe that many of the secret sorrows of woman's life, owe half their poignancy to the disappointment of not being able to obtain the degree of admiration which has been studiously sought. A popular and elegant writer has said—"How often do the wounds of our vanity form the secret of our pathos! " And to the situation, and the feelings of woman, this observation is more especially applicable. Still, there is much to be said for woman in this respect. By the nature of her own feelings, as well as by the established rules of polished life, she is thrown, as it were, upon the good-will of society. Unable to assert her own claims to protection, she must endeavour to ensure it by secondary means, and she knows that the protection of man is best ensured by recommending herself to his admiration.

Nor is this all. There is but a faint line of demarkation between admiration and love. Though essentially different in their nature, and not always called forth by the same individual, their outward aspect is still so much alike, and there is so frequent a transition made from the one to the other, that it requires more able reasoning than the generality of women are capable of, to know exactly when they are exciting admiration, and when they are inspiring love. There is, however, one infallible test by which the case may be decided, and I can- not too earnestly recommend to my countrywomen to apply it to themselves. If they are admired without being beloved, they may possibly be favourites in company abroad, but they will be no favourites at home—they may obtain the goodwill of a mere acquaintance, but they will be solitary and neglected at their own fireside. If they are cultivating such habits as are calculated to make them really beloved, especially at home, they may retire from company in which they have been wholly overlooked, to find the warmest welcome of the domestic circle awaiting their return—they may not be able to create any perceptible sensation when they appear in public, but every familar countenance around their social hearth will be lighted up with smiles when they appear.

With regard to the love of admiration, it is much to be regretted that all women who make this one of the chief objects of their lives, do not at the same time evince an equal solicitude to be admired for what is really praiseworthy. Were this the case, they would at least be employed in cultivating useful habits; and as the student who aims at obtaining a prize, even if he fails in that direct object, has obtained what is more desirable, in the power of application which he has made himself master of; so the woman who aims at moral excel- lence, if the taste of society is too vitiated to receive with admiration the first impression her character is calculated to make, has yet acquired such habits as will prove an inestimable treasure throughout the whole of her after life.

We do not, however, see that this is the case so much as might be desired in modern society. There is an appearance amongst the women of the present day, of being too eager for an immediate tribute of admiration, to wait for the developement of moral worth; and thus they cultivate those more shining accomplishments, which dazzle and delight for the moment, but leave no materials for agreeable reflection behind. Like the conducter of an exhibition of fire-works, they play off their splendid combinations of light and colour; but the magazine is soon expended, and the scene closes with weariness, and vacuity, and the darkness of night.

What a waste of time, and means, and application, for such a result! What an expenditure of thought and feeling, to have produced this momentary display! Surely no philanthropist can behold unmoved the pitiful objects for which women who court the incense of admiration, are spending their lives. Surely none of the patriot sons of Britain can look on, and see with indifference the sisters, the wives, the mothers, of our English homes, perpetually employed, even in a world of care and suffering, of anxiety and disappointment, in administering to the momentary gratification of the eye and the ear, while the heart is left unsatisfied, and the drooping soul uncheered.

The desire of being beloved is an ambition of a far more amiable and praiseworthy character. But who shall record the endless variety of suffering it entails upon woman? I will not believe of my sex, that it is the love of admiration only, which gives birth to all those rivalries and mortifications—that envy, and spleen, and bitterness, which mar the felicity of female companionship. It must be some deeper feeling; and I at least will give them credit for being wounded in a tenderer point than their vanity, before they can so far do violence to their gentler nature, as to revenge upon each other the slights and the humiliations they receive.

Yes: it is to human calculation the most pardonable, and yet it is the most soul-besetting sin of woman, to be perpetually investing earthly objects with an interest too intense for her own happiness; and asking of some oracle she has herself established, for an answer to the language of her own heart. Let her seek as she may, the admiration and applause of the world, it never satisfies the craving of her soul. She must have something to come home to—a shelter even in the brightest sunshine—a bower in the fairest garden—a shrine within the richest temple. She cannot mingle with the stream of life, and float securely on, as one amongst the many. She will not even be exalted in solitary distinction. The world has no wealth to offer, that she would possess alone.

This is the true nature of woman; and the home she seeks is in the hearts of those who are bound to her by affection. She knows that her place in this home is not to be maintained without unceasing care; and hence the solicitude she bestows upon things of trifling moment. She knows also that in some instances she is liable to be supplanted; she feels, perhaps, that she is not worthy to monopolize so honourable a place; and hence her watchfulness and jealousy. It may be that she is "discarded thence, " for human love is sometimes treacherous; and hence her wounded spirit, and the occasional outpouring of natural feeling, by which she brings upon herself the odium of bitterness and revenge.

Thus the darkest faults of woman may often be traced back to those peculiarities of her nature, which, under favouring circumstances, and with the Divine blessing, may constitute her highest recommendation, and surest source of happiness. How important is it, then, since to woman it is essential to be loved, that she should not expect to reap where she has never sown, and thus incur the most painful disappointment to which her suffering nature is liable!

With regard to the anxiety to be admired, then, I would propose that approve should be substituted for admire, and just so far as women seek the approval of their friends, under the guidance of religious truth, there is every reason to believe they will reap an abundant reward. With regard to the desire to be beloved, I can only repeat, that the women of England are peculiarly blessed in the means they possess of rendering themselves estimable in society; and the opportunities they enjoy of cultivating the kindest and happiest feelings of our nature. They have the homes of England in their keeping; and the hearts within those homes must necessarily be attracted or repelled by the light or the shade which their presence diffuses around them. They cannot complain that circumstances are against them in the attainment of moral worth. All the natural characteristics of their native country are in their favour. The happiness of the whole human family, and especially of man, supplies them with a never-failing motive. Nature and religion are both on their side—the one to prompt, the other to lure them on. They have the gratitude of their fellow-creatures awaiting their endeavours—and what is more, they have the gracious approval of their heavenly Father, as their encouragement and reward.

CHAPTER XII. PUBLIC OPINION—PECUNIARY RESOURCES—
INTEGRITY.

THE respect paid by women to public opinion, and to the
conventional rules of society, might have been considered with some
propriety under the head of love of admiration, did not the
immediate connexion of this subject with that of integrity, render it
more suited to the present CHAPTER.

To use a popular Germanism, it is but a one-sided view of the subject
that we take, when we suppose that the hope of being admired is the
strongest stimulus to the female character in all cases where her
conduct is referred to public opinion. The dread of being censured or
condemned, exercises, I am inclined to think, a far more extensive
influence over her habits and her feelings. Any deviation from the
fashionable mode of dress, or from the established usages of
polished life, present an appalling difficulty to a woman of ordinary
mind brought up under the tutelage of what is called the world. She
cannot—positively cannot—dare not—will not do any thing that the
world has pronounced unlady-like. Nor, while she lives in the
world, and mixes in polished society, is it at all desirable that she
should deviate from such universally acknowledged rules, except
where absolute duty leads her into a different line of conduct. I
should be the last person to advise a woman to risk the consequences
of such deviations, simply for the sake of being singular; because, I
regard the assumption of singularity for its own sake, as one of the
most absurd of all the varied specimens of affectation which human
life affords.

To choose to be singular without a sufficient reason, and to dare to
be so in a noble cause, are so widely different, that I desire to be
clearly understood in the remarks I am about to make, as referring
strictly to those cases in which duty renders it necessary for women
to deviate from the fashions and established customs of the time or
place in which they live.

While the tide of prosperity bears us smoothly on, and our means are
ample, and our luxuries abundant, we suffer little inconvenience
from the tyranny of the world in these respects. Indeed, it is rather
an agreeable amusement to many ladies to consult the fashions of
the day, and to be amongst the first to change their mode of dress—
to order costly furniture, and to receive company in the most

154

approved and lady-like style. But as I have before observed, of the class of persons to which this work chiefly relates, the tide of prosperity is apt to ebb, as well as to flow; and as it recedes from us, the whole aspect of the world is not only changed to us, but the aspect of our conduct is changed to the world; so that, what it approved in us before, and honoured with its countenance, is now the subject of its extreme and bitter condemnation.

It is then that we discover, we have been serving a hard master; but unfortunately for thousands of human beings, the discovery brings with it no freedom from that service. We loathe the cruel bondage; but habit is too strong for conviction, and we continue to wear the galling chain. It is, then, in cases of adverse fortune, that we see the incalculable benefit of having made the moral duties of social and domestic life the rule of our conduct, and of having regarded all outward embellishments as things of very subordinate importance.

It is a case of by no means rare occurrence, that the young women of England return home from school more learned in the modes of dress, and habits of conduct prevailing amongst the fashionable and the wealthy, than in any of those systems of intellectual culture in which they have been instructed. Or if their knowledge has not extended to what is done in fashionable life, they have at least learned to despise what is done amongst the vulgar and the poor, to look upon certain kinds of dress as impossible to be worn, and to regard with supreme contempt every indication of the absence of fashionable manners. So far as their means of information could be made to extend, they have laid down, for the guidance of their future lives, the exact rules by which the outward conduct of a lady ought to be regulated, and by these rules they determine to abide.

If this determination was applied exclusively to what is delicate, refined, and lovely in the female character, they would unquestionably be preparing themselves for being both esteemed and beloved; but unfortunately for them, their attention is too often directed to the mode of dress worn by per- sons much higher than themselves in worldly prosperity, and to all the minutiæ of look and manner which they regard as indications of easy circumstances, and exemption from vulgar occupation.

Nor is the school itself, or the mode of treatment there, to be regarded as the source of these ideas and conclusions. The customs of modern society, and the taste of modern times, are solely in fault.

And wherever young ladies are congregated together with the same means of communication as at school, the same results must follow, until the public taste undergoes a material change, or until the women of England have become learned in a higher school of wisdom.

With the preparation here alluded to, our young women enter upon social life; and as years roll on, the habits thus acquired of making custom and fashion the rule of their lives, strengthen with the establishment of their character, and become parts of their very being. What then is the consequence of such habits in the day of their adversity, when the diminution of their pecuniary means leaves them no longer the power of conforming to the world they have so loved? The consequence is, that along with many real privations, their ideal sufferings are increased a hundred-fold, by the fact that they must dress and live in a manner different from what they have been accustomed to—in short, that they must lose caste.

How little has the mere circumstance of relinquishing our luxuries to do with the distress attendant upon the loss of worldly substance. We find every day that persons travelling expressly for enjoyment, joining in social excursions, and even seeking the invigoration of their health, and the refreshment of their spirits, from the sea-breezes, or in places of customary resort for the summer months, voluntarily resign more than half their habitual indulgences, and subject themselves, without a murmur, to the occupation of apartments which they would scarcely think possible to be endured for a single day in their native town; and all the while they are perhaps more happy and more cheerful than in their elegant drawing-rooms at home.

It is evident, then, that it cannot be their individual share in the gratification of artificial wants, which they find it so heart-breaking to resign. It must be that a certain number of polite and refined individuals having combined to attach a high degree of importance to the means of procuring the luxuries of life, all who belong to this class, when compelled to exhibit in public a manifest destitution of such means, regard them- selves, and expect to be regarded by others, as having beome degraded in the sight of their fellow-creatures, and no longer entitled to their favour or regard.

It is of no use asserting that we all know better than to come to this conclusion—that mankind are not so weak, or so unjust—that we

156

appreciate the moral worth of an individual beyond the luxuries of his table, or the costliness of his dress. It is easy to say this; but it is not so easy to believe it, because the practical proof of experience is against it. If, for instance, we cared for none of these things, why should the aspect of human life present such a waste of time, and health, and patience, and mental power, and domestic peace, in the pursuit of wealth, when that wealth is expended, as soon as gained, in maintaining an appearance of elegance and luxury before the world?

I am not prepared to argue about the benefits resulting from the encouragement of artificial wants, and the increase of luxuries, on the broad scale of national prosperity. There are pens more able and more fit for such a purpose. My narrower views are confined to the individual evils resulting from an over-strained ambition to keep pace with our wealthier associates in our general habits; and I would write with earnestness on this subject, because I believe that in England, at the present time, these evils are of rapidly increasing extent.

It may seem unimportant to those who have no experience in these affairs, to speak of the private and domestic disputes arising out of artificial wants, on one side, and inability to provide the demanded supply for them, on the other. Yet what family, in moderate circumstances, has not some record of scenes, alike humiliating to human nature, and destructive to human happiness, in which the ill-judged request, or the harsh denial—the importunate appeal, or the agonizing reply—the fretful remonstrance, or the bitter retort, have not at seasons cast a shade over the domestic hearth, and destroyed the peace of the circle gathered around the social board.

It may appear still more like trifling, to speak of the sensations, with which a member of a fallen family regards her dilapidated wardrobe, and looks, and looks in vain for a garment sufficiently respectable to make her appearance in before a rich relation. Perhaps she has but one—a call has to be made upon a person of distinction, and as she proceeds on her way, eyeing with watchful anxiety every speck and spray that would be likely to reduce her garment below the average of respectability, a storm overtakes her. There are carriages for all who can afford to pay for them, but none for her: and the agony of losing her last claim to gentility takes possession of her soul.

The reader may possibly smile at the absurdity of this case. A half-clad savage from some barbarous island, would probably smile, could he be made to understand it. But nothing can be farther from exciting a smile than the real sensations it occasions. Nothing can be farther from a smile than the look with which a failing tradesman regards the forlorn condition of his hat, when he dares not brush it, lest he should render its destitution more apparent. Nothing can be farther from a smile, than the glance he casts upon his threadbare coat, when he knows of no possible resource in art or nature that can supply him with a new one. And nothing can be farther from a smile, than the cold welcome we give to a guest who presents himself unexpectedly, and must, perforce, look in upon the scantiness of our half-furnished table.

It is easy to class these sources of disquietude under the head of absurdities, and to call them unworthy of rational beings; but I do believe, there is more real misery existing in the world at the present time, from causes like these, than from all those publicly-acknowledged calamities which are more uniformly attributed to the dispensations of Providence.

I do not mean that these miseries arise directly from, or are by any means confined to, our personal appearance, or the furniture of our houses; but when we contemplate the failure of pecuniary means, as it is regarded by the world, and attempt to calculate the immense variety of channels through which the suffering it produces is made to flow, in consequence of the customs and habits of society, I believe they will be found to extend through every variety of human life, to the utmost range of human feeling. Is it not to escape this suffering that the man of unsound principles too frequently applies himself to dishonourable means—that the suicide prepares the deadly draught—and that the emigrant sometimes forsakes his native land, and consigns himself to the solitude of unpeopled wilds? —In short, what more remains within the range of human capability, which man has not done, with the hope of flying from the horrors attendant upon the falling away of his pecuniary means?

When the reality of this suffering is acknowledged, as it must be by all who look upon society as it exists at the present moment; the next subject of importance is, to consider how the suffering can be obviated, and its fatal effects upon the peace and happiness of society prevented.

The most immediate means that could be made to operate upon woman would unquestionably be, by implanting in her mind a deeper and more rational foundation of thought and feeling—to put a stop to that endless variety of ill-natured gossip which relates to the want of elegance, or fashionable air in certain persons' dress and manner of living; so that there should be no more questioning, "What will be thought of my wearing this dress again? " "What will Miss P., or Mrs. W. say, if they see our old curtains? " "What can the Johnsons mean by travelling outside? " "What will the people at church or chapel say, when they see your shabby veil? " "I positively don't believe the Wilsons can afford a new carpet, or they would surely have one; and they have discontinued their subscription to our book-society. "

It is neither grateful nor profitable to pursue these remarks any farther than as they serve for specimens of that most contemptible of small-talk, which yet exercises a powerful influence over the female mind—so much so, that I have known the whole fabric of a woman's philosophy entirely overthrown, and her peace of mind for the moment destroyed, by the simple question, whether she had no other dress than the one she was so often seen to wear.

There is another instance that occurs to me, as illustrating, in a striking manner, the subject immediately under consideration: it is that of wearing mourning for a deceased relative. This custom is so generally acknowledged as desirable, that it needs no recommendation from my pen. One would suppose, however, on a superficial view of it, that the wearing of black, as a general costume indicative of the absence of festivity or merriment from the bereaved family, was all that had been originally intended by this custom; and that it should thus become an outward testimony of respect and sorrow for the dead.

The fashion of the world, however, has imposed upon this custom, as applies to females, certain restrictions, and additions so expensive in their nature as to render it rather an article of luxury to wear genteel mourning, or that which is indicative of the deepest grief. It interferes but little with the sorrow and seclusion of a recent bereavement for the mistress of ample means to give orders for an external exemplification of precisely the degree of sorrow supposed to attend upon the loss of a parent, or a distant relative. but when the means of pecuniary expenditure are extremely small, and the materials for appearing properly in public have to be made up at home, and prepared for use within a very limited time, it is evident that greater regard to the sacredness of sorrow would suggest the desirableness of a less elaborate style of dress, or perhaps a dress not absolutely new for the occasion. Ladies, however, and those who have been accustomed to make gentility the primary rule of their conduct, must mourn genteelly; and, consequently, there are often scenes of bustling preparation, of invention, and studious arrangement—scenes, upon which, if a stranger should look in, he would see an appearance of activity, and interest, almost amounting to amusement, in the very house where the shutters are still closed; and which are wholly at variance with the silence and the sanctity of a deep and solemn grief.

Nor is this all. So extremely becoming and ladylike is the fashionable style of mourning, that, under the plea of paying greater respect to the memory of the dead, it has become an object of ambition to wear it in its greatest excellence; and equally an object of dread, and source of humiliation, to be compelled to wear it in an inferior style. Thus, when the loss of a father is attended with the failure of his pecuniary resources, it adds no little to the grief into which his daughters are plunged, to be under the necessity of appearing so soon after their twofold loss, under such an outward sign of poverty as is generally understood by the world to be betrayed by cheap and humble mourning.

It is evident that if the preparation of mourning had never been reduced to a system—so many folds of crape for a parent—so many for a sister, and so on—the peculiar style in which it might be made up would never have obtained half its present importance, and respectable women, of fallen fortunes, might then have appeared in public with the credit of paying as much honour to the memory of the dead, as the more wealthy; nay, they might even have been so absorbed in their heart-rending loss, and in all the solemn and affecting impressions it was calculated to inspire, as to forget to have any new preparation for the occasion, and might, without loss of respectability, appear again in those accustomed habiliments of darkness and gloom which former instances of family affliction and bereavement had been the means of bringing into use.

I mention the instance of mourning, not because it differs materially from many others, but because it appears to me to illustrate clearly and strikingly the degree of shame, and trouble, and perplexity, in which women are involved by the habit of attaching too much importance to the usages of society. I know that it is beneficial to the character and the morals of women, that their good name should be guarded from every breath of reproach; and that the wholesome restrictions of society are absolutely necessary to prevent them from sometimes venturing too far under the influence of generous and disinterested feeling. But my remarks apply exclusively to cases where their moral worth would be established, not endangered; and I would earnestly request my countrywomen to bear in mind the immense difference between deviating from the rules of fashion, and breaking through the wholesome restrictions of prudence.

I have spoken in strong terms of the sufferings and inconveniences incident to women, from their slavery to the opinion of the world; but were this consideration all that had to be taken into account, they would unquestionably have a right to adjust the balance, and act according to their own choice.

There is, however, a far more important question connected with this subject—and that is, the question of integrity.

If there be one moral quality for which England as a nation is distinguished above all others, I should say it was her integrity— integrity in her intercourse with other nations—integrity in the administration of her government and laws—integrity in the sound hearts and honourable feelings of her patriotic sons.

And shall her daughters be less solicitous to uphold this high standard of moral worth? They answer "No! " But they are perhaps not all aware of the encroaching and insidious nature of artificial wants, and tastes, and habits, founded upon the fashion of the times, rather than upon any lasting principle of right. They are not all aware, that to dress and live beyond their means, is a species of public robbery; and that even if every lawful debt is paid, and the balance struck without injury to character or credit, there are still the poor—the starving, hungry, helpless poor—unsatisfied with bread. They have therefore the strong claims, both of justice and benevolence, to fulfil, before the integrity of their christian character can be complete.

With regard to general benevolence, and charity to the poor, we are apt to deceive ourselves to an extent which would be beyond our belief, were we not convinced by the observation of every day, that few—very few of those even in the middle ranks of life—few even of those tender-hearted females who are so painfully affected by every exhibition of human misery, do anything at all commensurate with their means, towards alleviating the suffering which is to be found amongst the poor.

I am not inclined to attach any high degree of merit to the mere act of giving money to the poor, because I esteem it a luxury to be thus instrumental in relieving their pressing difficulties; and I am also in considerable doubt whether this is the best method of relieving them. The point I am about to remark upon, however, is the extreme inconsistency of those longings, so prevalent amongst ladies, that they could give to the poor; and the lamentations they frequently utter relating to the absolute necessity they are under, of not giving more. We find them elegantly dressed, dwelling amongst costly furniture, and denying themselves nothing which their wealthier neighbours enjoy—and all the while, they do so wish they could give more to the poor!

I confess it sickens the heart, and wearies the mind, to listen to absurdities like this. If these individuals would but let the matter rest, and be content to be fashionable without pretending to be generous, half their culpability would cease to exist. But they go on to explain to you how their station in life, and their credit in society, require them to dress and live in a certain way; and how they consider themselves doing a benefit to their country by their encouragement of its manufactures. It would not be inappropriate to ask them, as they enter a fashionable and expensive establishment to purchase some costly articles of dress, whether they are doing it in reality for the benefit of their country? and there might be seasons when it would be equally appropriate to inquire, whether they prefer their appearance before the world, to the spiritual consolation of having made the injunctions of their blessed Saviour the rule of their conduct.

The measure of charity, which it is our duty to bestow upon the poor, is a point of very difficult adjustment, as well as the manner we may choose to adopt in the distribution of our means. We cannot properly make ourselves the judge of a brother or a sister, in these respects. But if we have sufficient resources for the purchase of luxuries, it is in vain to pretend that we cannot give to the poor; and if we will not spare a little out of our little, we cannot expect to be believed, when we boast of the pleasure it would afford us to be charitable with more.

There are noble instances afforded by women in the middle classes of society in England, of what can really be done in the way of benevolence, in a persevering and unobtrusive manner, which it is truly refreshing to the soul to contemplate. And I would earnestly recommend my young countrywomen to look seriously to these, and to ask whether they cannot go and do likewise; rather than to accustom themselves to the dangerous habit of inquiring whether they cannot afford to purchase what is fashionable and becoming to a lady, even when it is not necessary for comfort or respectability. By this means they would at least be able to attain a degree of merit; for if they did not go to the extent of the truly devoted and praiseworthy, they might avoid involving themselves in that interminable chain of expensive contingencies, which are sure to follow, if we set out in life by making it our first object of ambition to stand well with the world, and to accommodate our dress and mode of living to that which is most admired in society.

The fallacious mode of reasoning induced by too slavish a conformity to the fashions and the customs of the world, creates an endless series of entanglements most fatally seductive to woman's better feelings. The fact of having, or not having, absolute debts unpaid, seems to be, with most young ladies, the boundary-line of their morality, as relates to their pecuniary affairs; and well would it be if all were strictly scrupulous even to this extent. Within this line, however, there may be deviations from the integrity of a noble, generous, and enlightened mind, which yet the world takes no cognizance of, and which do not materially affect the character, as it is judged of by society in general.

I have said that the world is an unjust judge; and in no instance is it more so than in this. The world pays homage to an expensive, elegant, and lady-like appearance; but it takes little note of the principle that would condemn this appearance, if it could not be maintained without encroachment upon a parent's limited means. The restrictions of civil law refer only to the payment of pecuniary debts; and when these are discharged, we may appear without reproach before society. But happily for us, we have a higher standard of moral duty; and the integrity of the christian character requires a strict observance of points of conduct unseen by society, and perhaps known only to ourselves, and to the great Searcher of human hearts, by whose judgment we must stand or fall.

Reasoning, then, upon these subjects, from higher principles, we clearly perceive that we have no right to indulge ourselves with luxuries, or to purchase the countenance and favour of society, at the expense of a parent's peace, or by the sacrifice of the comforts of his old age. We have no right to encroach upon means not strictly and lawfully our own, even though they should be granted to our necessities, for more than belongs to actual decency of appearance, and sufficiency of subsistence, except in those cases where it is the desire of wealthy friends or relatives that we should be adorned and supplied at their expense. We have no right, and no woman of good feeling would wish to establish a right, to dress and live at the extreme of expenditure, which a father, by nothing less than hourly and incessant toil, can obtain the means of affording. We have no right to make presents, and thus obtain the meed of gratitude and admiration for our generosity, with money which is immediately transmitted from our father's hand for that especial purpose, while our own resources remain undiminished, our own pri- vate store of treasures uninvaded, and our circumstances wholly unaffected.

I do not say that to each one of the immense variety of daily and familiar actions, which might be classed under this head, there attaches the highest degree of actual culpability. They are rather instances of encroachment, than of absolute injustice and wrong. But I do say that the habit of encroaching, just so far as decency will permit, and as occasion seems to warrant, upon all that is noble and generous, upright and kind, in human conduct, has a fatal tendency to corrupt the heart, while it produces at the same time a deadening effect upon the highest and holiest aspirations of the soul.

What answer can be made by such a soul to the secret questionings of its internal monitor? Or how shall we appeal to the gracious and merciful Creator of the universe, who has given us all this glorious world for our enjoyment, and all the elements of nature for our use; who has looked upon us in our degradation, and pitied our infirmities, and opened the gates of heaven, that his mercy might descend to us in a palpable and human form, and that we might receive the conditions of his offered pardon, be healed, and live? — how shall we appeal to him in our private prayers, or stand before him in the public sanctuary, with this confession on our lips—that just so far as man could approve or condemn our actions, we have deemed it expedient to be just; but that to him, and to the Saviour of our souls, we have grudged the incense of a willing mind; and therefore we have enhanced our pleasures, and gratified our pride, and fed our selfishness, by all those trifling, yet forbidden means, which he has pronounced to be offensive in his sight?

Besides these considerations, there is one of immeasurable importance, connected with our conduct in the sight of God. No human mind can set a bound, or prescribe a measure, to its voluntary deviations from the line of duty. We have been supposing a case in which these deviations are extremely minute, and yet so numerous as to form as it were a circle round the heart—a circle of evil. Imagine, then, this circle widening, and widening, year after year, through the seasons of youth and maturity, and the dreary winter of old age. What an awful and melancholy spectacle does the state of that heart present, enclosed as it were in a deleterious atmosphere, and growing perpetually colder and more callous by exclusion from the blessed light of heaven.

Oh! let us not begin to breathe this deadly atmosphere! And you who are yet inexperienced in the ways of human life, whose habits are not formed, whose paths not chosen, whose line of conduct not decided, what a blessing would it be to you, both in this world and in the world to come, were you to choose that better part, that would enable you to look with a single eye to what is most acceptable in the Divine sight, and most in accordance with the will of God; leaving the embellishments of person, the luxuries of taste, and the appropriation of worldly esteem, to be enjoyed or relinquished with a grateful and contented mind, just as your heavenly Father may permit; and bearing always about with you, as a talisman against the encroachments of evil, even in the most simple or most specious form, the remembrance that none of these things are worthy of a single wish, if they must necessarily be obtained by the violation of his laws, or accompanied by the tokens of his displeasure.

CHAPTER XIII. HABITS AND CHARACTER—INTELLECTUAL ATTAINMENTS—EMPLOYMENT OF TIME—MORAL COURAGE—RIGHT BALANCE OF MIND.

TO those gentle readers, who have been kind enough to accompany me through the foregoing pages, and who feel inclined to exercise their forbearance through a few more, I feel that some apology, or rather some explanation, is necessary for the manner in which I have so often been compelled to speak of the extraordinary ambition manifested by my countrywomen, in the present day, to make themselves mistress of every possible variety of intellectual attainment that can be acquired at school; and I cannot help fearing, that many of my remarks may appear to have been written with a view to depreciate the value of these treasures of mind, and, as far as my single influence may extend, to deter others from the pursuit of them.

So far from this, I would repeat, if possible, in words which could not be forgotten, my firm conviction, that no human being can learn too much, so that their sphere of intelligence does not extend to what is evil. But, while the accumulation of a vast store of knowledge is one of the objects we have in view in the culture of the mind, we must not forget that it is by no means the only one. In rearing an infant, we not only supply its appetite with food, but also find it necessary to teach it the habit, and assist it in the power, of exercising its limbs; we guide its steps, and, as far as we are able, give it just notions of exercising its bodily functions with the best effect.

To feed the mind, then, is but a small part of our duty. If we leave it helpless and inert, without ability to exercise its various powers, and judgment to exercise them aright, the most important portion of that duty is neglected. Thus far, I believe, all who are employed in teaching the young, will go along with me, for their experience must afford strong evidence in favour of this statement. There are some points, however, in which, it appears to me, they have allowed the fashion of the times to render their system of instruction extremely defective. But, for this, I am by no means prepared to say, that they are in any degree to blame; because they have the taste of the times to consult; and, they would obtain little credit for making our young women what they ought to be, if that taste was not correct.

With regard to moral discipline, or that mode of instruction by which women would be fitted for their domestic and social duties, I have expressed my opinion in an earlier CHAPTER of this work; and, with regard to intellectual culture, I hope to be pardoned if I now venture a few remarks.

It appears to me, in looking abroad upon society, and contemplating the immense variety of mental attainments which prevail amongst the young women of the present day, that they are in imminent danger of supposing, when they have acquired a vast amount of verbal knowledge, that the great work of education is done. They are, in short, in danger of mistaking the means for the end; and of resting satisfied that they are wiser than the generation before them.

In the acquirement of languages, this is particularly the case. A young lady obtains the reputation of being clever, when she has made herself mistress of several languages; and with this she is generally satisfied; while she ought to remember that she has but gained possession, as it were, of the keys of vast storehouses of knowledge, for the use of which she is responsible to society.

Our young ladies are made acquainted while at school, with the dates of most of the leading events of history, with the years when certain kings began to reign, and the precise time of their holding the reins of government. The various devices for impressing these events upon their recollection, are no less ingenious than commendable; but could any plan be adopted for enabling them to draw conclusions from such facts, to compare historical events with each other, to trace the progress of civilization, and to ascertain what circumstances have most invariably led to the rise or the fall of different empires— instead of being confined to isolated facts, their conversation would then be fraught with the richer burden of those important truths, for which history supplies nothing more than illustration.

Again, in the pursuit of science, there is a technicality that strikes the ear, and gives an idea of vast superiority in the way of attainments; and there are facts that may be impressed upon the memory, without the mind being in any way enlarged, or enlightened by the reception of them. It is easy, for instance, to talk of botany, without the thoughts at any time extending themselves to the general economy of vegetation; and of astronomy, so as to tell the distances of different planets, without the soul being penetrated by one ray of illumination from the wisdom which designed, and which controls the starry heavens. It is easy to attend a few scientific lectures, and to return home talking of the names of gases, and of some of the most striking phenomena of electricity, the galvanic battery, and other popular exhibitions of the lecture-room; but it requires a totally different process of mind, to take a general survey of the laws of the universe, and to bow before the conviction that all must have been created by a hand divine.

From our observations of rural or romantic scenery, it is easy to babble about woods and waterfalls, about the ruggedness of mountains, and the grandeur of the raging sea; but it does not follow as a necessary consequence that we have formed any conception of the idea of abstract beauty, or of the reverential, but admiring awe, which true sublimity is calculated to inspire. It does not follow that we shall have learned to embody in the elements of nature, those subtler essences of spirit and of mind, which, to the poetical and imaginative, people every desert, and render vocal with melody the silence of night.

It may be said, that in this busy world, there is little employment for the imagination—little scope for the exercise of poetical associations. I grant—for I am compelled to do so—that poetry should be elbowed out of our working world to make room for machinery; but I see no reason why the same train of thought, and course of reasoning, should not be carried on. I grant that the materials are different; but why should we not still endeavour to raise an altar in our minds for a higher, holier worship than that of the mammon of this world? Why should we fix our attention solely upon the material part of the universe, satisfying ourselves with the names of substantial things, with their variety, classification, and physical properties? Why should we confine ourselves to counting the pillars in the temple of nature, computing its magnitude and measuring its height, without referring our calculations, through the highest range of imagination, to the wonder-working power of the great Artificer?

It may be said, that we dwell too much in cities, and lead too artificial a life, to be able to perceive the instrumentality of Divine Wisdom in all the events that pass beneath our observation. If this be the case, there is the more need that we should rouse ourselves by fresh efforts, to penetrate beyond the polished surface of the world in which we live, into the deeper mysteries that lie beyond—there is the more need that we should endeavour to perceive, in the practical affairs of busy life, those great principles by which the laws of nature are governed, and the system of the universe upheld.

If, for instance, we live in the heart of a thickly-peopled city, with the rush of its busy multitudes around us, and the labour of man's hand, and the efforts of his ingenuity, perpetually before our eyes, there is no reason why we should look only at the splendour of its manufactured articles, amuse our fancy with the outward aspect of its varied exhibitions of art, or regard with disgust the occupations of the mechanic, because he handles the raw material, and touches what is gross. Would it not be more consistent with the exercise of an enlightened mind, to contemplate the wonders of that power which the Creator has entrusted to the use of man, so that he lays hold, as it were, of the elements of nature, and makes them submit to his will?

Night falls not with stillness and repose upon the city, but we walk as through a living blaze: and shall we pass on, like children, pleased with the glitter and the show, without reflecting that man has been able to convert the darkest substance from the bowels of the earth into the very source of all this light? Mountains and valleys, tracts of land and floods of water, intervene between us and our distant friends; but we fly to them with a rapidity, which, a few years ago, would have been pronounced, even by philosophers, impossible. And shall we move like senseless matter, even through the very heart of the mountain, calculating only the speed at which we travel, without awaking to the momentous fact, that by the ingenuity of man, mere vapour, proverbial as it is for its weakness, emptiness, and nothingness in the creation, has been converted into the master-power by which the mighty operations of men are carried on. We take our daily walks through the bustling city, and gaze at the splendid exhibitions of taste, and learn the names of those who are most skilled in music and painting, and all the sister arts; and we speak in the cant terms that are most in vogue, and think we display superiority of mind and intelligence to use them well; but should we not at the same time cultivate the habit of bearing in remembrance the unchanging principles of beauty, and of referring back to them whatever is offered to our admiration in the form of art?

We speak of the degrading cares and sordid views that occupy the working world; but how have we endeavoured to pass beyond these, and to connect them with the world of thought? We hear of the vast amount of labour carried on, and the relative expenses incurred, and the different things that can be made and done within a given time:

but why should we not sometimes make a transition of thought from the material, to the means of working it—from the means, to the power—and from the power that is imparted, to the Creator who imparts. To-day the mechanic plies his busy tools. To-morrow his hand may have become rigid and motionless beneath the stroke of death. Thousands and tens of thousands pass away from the scene of their labours, but the labour still goes on; for the laws of nature change not, and the principles upon which the labour of man is carried into effect, remain the same.

As with one accord, our young ladies appear to have come to the determination of dismissing from their minds even the faintest apprehension of the subject of political economy, except when garnished to their taste by an attractive story; nor could this be wondered at, were the subject necessarily associated with the vulgarity of party politics. But they seem to forget that the coarse jargon of popular excitement, has little to do with the spirit of their country's laws, the policy of her negociations, the benevolence and wisdom of her institutions; and the principles of justice by which her integrity is upheld. A little attention properly bestowed upon these subjects would enable women, not only to converse with men upon some of their favourite themes; but what is of more importance, to lead them away by imperceptible degrees, from those partial views which are the result of prejudice, those violent expressions which ignorance alone can justify, and that personality of remark so destructive to the peace and good will of society.

We are too apt, because we mingle in populous and busy scenes, and feel the necessity of moving with the tide, to forget that what we see and hear, what is obvious to the senses and palpable to the touch, is not all that we live for, or even all that we live amongst. We should endeavour to find breathing-times even amidst the hurry and the rush of present things. We should sometimes pause amongst the multitude, and listen mentally, to the beating of the mighty pulse of a tumultuous city, and ask, whether the Creator and Sustainer of this living mass is not beholding the operation of the various powers he has set in motion, marking its defects, supplying its deficiences, and sustaining the stupendous whole. We should then be enabled to perceive something of the working of the inner plan, how one class of human beings depends upon another—how the principles of justice establish checks and counter-checks, so that no single power shall be predominant; how poverty and riches alternate, and how the vices of the bad are made to call forth the virtues of the good; and by renewing our conviction that God is indeed here, as well as present to the more peaceful and harmonious portions of his creation, we should renew our faith, and enjoy perpetual refreshment for our souls.

What we most want in education, then, is to invest material things with the attributes of mind; and we want this more and more, as commerce, and arts, and manufactures increase in importance and extent. We want it more and more, to give interest to our familiar and necessary occupations; and we want it, especially, that we may assist in redeeming the character of English men from the mere animal, or rather, the mere mechanical state, into which, from the nature and urgency of their occupations, they are in danger of falling.

We want it also for ourselves; for a time seems to be approaching, when the middle class of society in England will have to be subdivided; and when the lower portion of this class will of necessity have to turn their attention to a different style of living, and to different modes of occupation, thought, and feeling. At present all this class are educated nearly upon the same plan. The happiness of society, and our moral necessities, will surely, before long, suggest the importance of females of this class being fitted for something very different from drawing-room exhibitions.

All that I have written in this volume, imperfect as it is, has been stimulated by a desire to increase the moral worth of my countrywomen, and enhance the domestic happiness of my native land. In order that this should be done effectually, it seems to me indispensably necessary, that women, whose parents are possessed of slender means, or engaged in business, and who can with extreme difficulty accomplish even so much as what is called "making their way,"—that women in this class should be educated, not simply for ladies, but for useful and active members of society—and for this purpose, that they also should consider it no degradation to render their activity conducive to the purposes of trade.

It is a curious anomaly in the structure of modern society, that gentlemen may employ their hours of business in almost any degrading occupa- tion, and, if they have but the means of supporting a respectable establishment at home, may be gentlemen still; while, if a lady does but touch any article, no matter how delicate, in the way of of trade, she loses caste, and ceases to be a lady.

I say this with all possible respect for those who have the good sense and the moral courage to employ themselves in the business of their fathers and their husbands, rather than to remain idle and dependent; because I know that many of them are ladies in the best acceptation of the word—ladies in the delicacy and propriety of their feelings, and more than ladies in the noble dignity of their general conduct. Still I doubt not they have had their difficulties to encounter from the influence of public opinion, and that their generous feelings have been often wounded by the vulgar prejudices prevailing in society against their mode of life.

With the improvements of art, and the increase of manufactures, there must be an increased demand for mechanics and work-people of every description; and supposing English society to be divided, as it soon must be, into four classes, there surely can be no reason why the second class of females should not be so trained, as to partake in the advantages resulting from this extended sphere of active and useful occupation. —The only field at present open for what is considered lady-like employment, is that of educating the young; and hence the number of accomplished young women, too refined for common usefulness, whose claims to public attention as governesses tend so much to reduce the value of their services in that important sphere.

There are, however, many descriptions of occupation connected with business in its varied forms, which are by no means polluting to the touch, or degrading to the mind; and it would be an unspeakable advantage to hundreds of young females, if, instead of useless accomplishments, they could be instructed in these. In addition to all kinds of fancy millinery, the entire monopoly of which they might surely be permitted to enjoy, I would point out especially to their attention, the art of engraving, which might very properly call into exercise the taste and ingenuity of the female sex, without taxing too severely their mental or bodily powers. To this I would add, the art of drawing patterns for the muslin and calico printers, an occupation which appears peculiarly adapted to the female taste, and which might be carried on without the least encroachment upon the seclusion of domestic life, and the delicacy of the female character. I have been led to understand that this branch of business is almost exclusively carried on by men; and I cannot but regret, that an employment, which offers a tempting luxury to those who suffer from the combined evils of idleness and scanty means, should not also be rendered productive of pecuniary benefit to women.

It seems, however, to be from this pecuniary benefit that they shrink; for when we observe the nature of their daily occupations, their common stitchery, their worsted work, their copied music, their ingeniously-invented articles for bazaars, it should be difficult to say in what sense they are more agreeable, or more dignified, than many branches of art connected with trade. It must therefore be the fact of receiving money for what they do, which renders the latter so objectionable; and it is a strange paradox in our daily experience, that this money should all the while be the very thing of which they are most in want.

The degradation of what is vulgarly called making their own living, is, I believe, the obstacle of paramount difficulty; and therefore it is to reduce this difficulty, and to render it more easily surmountable, that our solicitude for the well-being of society, with all our influence, and all our talent, ought to be employed.

It is in vain to argue in such cases, that individuals have no right to think and feel as they do—that women ought to be wiser than to consider themselves degraded by working for their own subsistence; while such is the constitution of society, and such the early bias of the female mind, that it is almost impossible they should do otherwise. The great point to be gained, is to penetrate at once to the root of the matter, and to begin by a different system of education, to render moral courage—the courage to do what is right—the first principle of female conduct.

What a world of misery this single principle of action, thoroughly grafted into the character, would spare the sons and daughters of men!

I am inclined to think the foundation of moral courage must be laid in very early life, so as to render it effectual in bearing us up under the trials of maturer age; and it is not only to elevate the general character of my countrywomen, but to spare them at least half the sufferings they now endure, that I would most earnestly recommend them, in cultivating the mind, to cultivate also the inestimable power of exercising moral courage, whenever the claims of duty are set in opposition to the opinions of the world.

For want of moral courage, how many misun- derstandings do we leave unsettled amongst our friends, until, "The lightly uttered, careless word, " the thoughtless action, or the false report, are allowed to poison the very springs of affection, and to separate the dearest friends. For want of moral courage, how often, and how fatally, do we fail in the sacred duty of reproving what we see amiss, until the evil grows, and magnifies, and extends itself, and becomes so obvious to general perception, that we scruple not to join in its condemnation, forgetting that our own want of faithfulness may possibly be chargeable with its existence.

For want of moral courage, how do we sink, and see others sinking every day, under the pressure of those pecuniary difficulties which I have already described, until we are guilty of almost every species of paltry meanness, to support an appearance of respectability before the world, forgetting that the grand foundation of all respectability of character, is an honourable, independent, and upright mind. For want of moral courage, how often do we stoop and cringe, and submit to contumely, and eat the bread of humiliation, and wear the rich garments that ought to cover us with shame, because we are despicable enough to live upon what is not lawfully our own, and what is often granted without good-will, and received without satisfaction.

Oh! that the women of England would rouse themselves with one accord, to break these galling chains! —to exemplify in their own conduct, and to teach their daughters, that there is no earthly enjoyment, no personal embellishment, no selfish gratification, worth the sacrifice of just and honourable feeling—that the humblest occupation, undertaken from a sense of duty, becomes ennobled in the motive by which it is prompted, and that the severest self-denial may be blessed and honoured by the Father of mercies, if endured in preference to an infringement upon those laws which he has laid down for the government of the human family.

There is another point of view, in which it appears to me that the present character of the women of England is extremely defective. It is as regards a right balance of mind; or, in other words, a just estimate of the relative importance of things in general.

From the natural construction of the mind of woman, from the quickness of her perceptions, and the intensity of her momentary feelings, she is apt to lay hold of every thing calculated immediately to strike her fancy, or to excite her emotions, with an earnestness that excludes the possibility of her mind being kept alive to other impressions, even more essential to her happiness, and more important in themselves.

Hence we find in society, that women too frequently invest the affairs of the moment, the circumstances occurring around them, and their own personal experience, with a degree of interest wholly incomprehensible to strangers, and often utterly contemptible to men. I do not—I will not believe—that women are inferior to what is called the noble sex, in the moral world; but I do believe that from this very cause arises more than half the contumely bestowed upon their littleness of character. It is not that they want capacity or understanding to judge of many things as well as men. It is that they are so occupied with what is obvious on the surface of things, that they will not look beyond; and hence their unceasing propensity to trifle, and to render themselves apparently inferior to what they really are.

This is the great leading defect in woman's character; and it is the more to be regretted, that it presents to her mind innumerable sources of disquietude, which with a more correct perception of the relative value of things, she might escape. She is apt, for instance, to attach as much importance, for the time, to the failure of her own musical performance, as to the failure of a bank; and she appears to care little for the invasion of a foreign country, when injury is threatened to her best attire. It is no trifling humiliation to those who mix in society, if they have been accustomed to raise their views a little higher in the contemplation of nature and of human life, to be perpetually persecuted, in the midst of agreeable and intelligent conversation, with questions about the minutiæ of dress and conduct in some limited and local sphere of observation.

I would not speak thus contemptuously of the familiar habits of my sex, if I did not know that they were capable of something better, and if I did not desire—as I desire their good and their happiness—that they would rouse themselves above this paltry littleness, and learn to become, what I am confident they might be, not only equal, but interesting and instructive companions to men.

I have before remarked, that there is now, more than ever, a demand for the exercise of their highest powers, and their noblest energies, to counteract the effects of unremitting toil in obtaining the perishing things of this life. There is a greater demand than ever upon their capabilities of enhancing social and domestic happiness; and there is an equal demand for the exercise I have already recommended, of the power they possess of investing what is material with the attributes of mind.

The littleness of character I have just described, is one of the chief causes why they are not so estimable as they might be in their homes, or so interesting as they are capable of being in their conversation with men. And thus their husbands and their brothers are becoming increasingly attracted by the political associations, and the public calls, now leading them away from those domestic scenes which offer little to excite the attention, or fascinate the mind.

It may be said, that English women in the present day are, in this respect at least, superior to the generation before them. But granting that they are so, the necessity for further improvement remains the same, because the habits of men are progressively involving them more deeply in the interests of public life; so that unless some strenuous efforts are made on the part of women, the far-famed homes of England will lose their boasted happiness, and with their happiness, their value in the scale of our country's moral worth.

This is a serious subject, and one which ought to appeal to every mother's bosom throughout our favoured land. It ought to be the solemn inquiry of every woman who has the sacred duty of training up the young committed to her trust, in what manner she may best guard against this growing evil, so as to stem the desolating tide which seems to threaten our domestic peace.

Let her, then, after this solemn inquiry has been made, endeavour to place herself in idea in the situation of a traveller who ascends a mountain, and look upon the varied aspects of human life as he regards the scene presented to his view. At first he will be struck with the magnitude of the rock he is climbing, amused perhaps with the plants that creep along its surface, and astonished with the opening out of distant valleys, and broad rivers rolling between other hills, amongst which his eye had never penetrated before. He advances a little higher, and sees other views extending far and wide, and the pinnacle of rock he at first thought so stupendous, diminishing beneath his feet—higher still, and the broad river, with its sweeping tide, has shrunk into a silver thread—still higher, and the pinnacle of rock is imperceptible, and he feels at last that he has gained the actual summit of the highest mountain, where he can compare the real height and distances of objects, and perceive how limited in comparison was the line which formed the original boundary of his vision—how small and low, and comparatively contemptible, the highest eminence to which he had then ascended.

It is in this manner that we ought to accustom ourselves to realize those views of human life, and that estimate of sublunary things, that would bring all to the standard of their real worth.

Judged of by this process, and tried by this rule, how differently should we appreciate the ordinary and familiar affairs of life. How little should we find to occupy our thoughts, or engage our affections, in the trifles that now constitute the actual business of our lives—how much should we find to admire and value in what we now despise!

It is to mothers, especially, that I would recommend this method of adjusting the balance of the infant mind, because the longer the weights are allowed to remain unequal, and the balance untrue, the more extensive must be the evil resulting from the erroneous data upon which the youthful mind will reason. And let them remember, that while the mistakes of their management will probably be exhibited more strikingly in the conduct of their sons, their daughters will extend the evil to a wider range of operation, by instilling it again into the minds of another generation.

It is not through a lifetime only, though that were sufficient for our follies—it may be through the endless ages of eternity, that our good or evil influence shall extend. I have pointed out to my countrywomen, as I pursued this work, the high ambition of preserving a nation from the dangers which threaten the destruction of its moral worth; but beyond this view, wide and exalted as it unquestionably is, there opens out a field of glory, upon which to enter might seem blessedness enough. Yet, when we contemplate the possibility of being the means of inducing others to enter with us, and those the most beloved of earth's treasures, surely it is worthy of our best energies—our most fervent zeal—our tears—our prayers—that we may so use our influence, and so employ our means, as that those whose happiness has been committed to our care, may partake with us in the enjoyment of the mansions of eternal rest.

Lightning Source UK Ltd.
Milton Keynes UK
UKOW040707030413

208597UK00001B/100/P